Meditating through the
BIBLE

REDISCOVER THE POWERFUL PERSPECTIVE TO LIFE

PARDON KANGARA

© 2024 Pardon Kangara.

No part of this publication may be reproduced, distributed, or transmitted in any form or by any means, including photocopying, recording, or other electronic or mechanical methods, without the prior written permission of the publisher, except in the case of brief quotations used in reviews and certain other noncommercial uses permitted by copyright law.

ISBN: 979-8-9917106-0-2

Cover Design: Asif Arain
Interior Book Design: www.wildwordsformatting.com
Editing: info@myeagleservices.com

Index of the BIBLE VERSIONS
REFERENCED IN THIS BOOK

In this book, attempt has been made to acknowledge the Bible version from which every highlighted Bible verse is quoted. Please reference the table below for your need.

Abbreviation	Bible Version
AMPC	The Amplified Bible Classic Edition
KJV	King James Version
NKV	New King James Version
ASV	American Standard Version
NIV	New International Version
BSB	Berean Standard Bible
ESV	English Standard Version
NRSV	New Revised Standard Version
NASB	New American Standard Bible
CSB	Christian Standard Bible
RSV	Revised Standard Version
NLT	New Living Translation
HCSB	Holman Christian Standard Bible
MSG	The Message Bible
BBE	The Bible in Basic English
NAB	New American Bible
TLB	The Living Bible

Dedication

To God, the Almighty, and My Father

All Glory belongs to you! Thank You for creating, loving, and blessing me. Thank you for sending Jesus, the Christ, to die for me. Words cannot utter my gratitude, nor can any vocalization equal it.

Thank you for inspiring me to search through the Scriptures and write this book. May it be a blessing to your creation.

I dedicate this book and the reader to you. Be glorified! I love You. Amen

To Elenah

I love you. You are a great daughter and princess of God. You are a great daughter of God and an individual who is supportive, insightful, and innovative. A faithful disciple of Jesus ministering to many. You are a virtuous wife and a blessing to me and our children. You are a mother in this Zion. I see the supernal grace of God in you every moment. You are such an immeasurable blessing to me!

Thank you for rediscovering the power of meditation through the voice of God. May God continue to bless you and enlarge your territory. I am excited to see together the unfolding future ahead.

I love and honor you. Amen.

To Yeve and Muno

Thank you for being born as my children. Thank you for your love and support. Take this as a letter and an admonition, perpetual in nature and an instrument to greatness.

May you do the greater works spoken of Jesus. Excel immeasurably. I love you. Amen.

To My Parents

I am grateful to my father, Cornelius, and my mother, Isabel.

I honor, love, and pray for you that God may enlarge you. God bless you. Amen.

To the Reader

I am taking this book as a seed I am planting in the ground. If you are reading this dedication and eventually this book, I have intentionally spoken a blessing for you before and during the time of writing. May it be yours if you can receive it. May the fruitfulness God intended with this inspiration make you fruitful in all you do. Through this book, let's discover for ourselves lifestyle practices that usher us to greater and unimaginable dimensions into the realities of His goodness and love.

I pray that God lets it be so in your life and that of your loved ones. In Jesus Christ's name, let it come forth. Amen.

Suggested Further READING

Supernal Grace by Elenah Kangara:

Having been part of the journey when Supernal Grace was written, I highly recommend this book.

Here is a link to the book: www.amazon.com/dp/B01N9NID7M

Be Blessed.

Leave a REVIEW
AND THANK YOU IN ADVANCE

After you read this book, I would appreciate it if you could leave a book review on Amazon.com. Simply visit the link below and you will be directed to the review page for *Meditating Through The Bible- Rediscover The Powerful Perspective to Life.*

https://www.amazon.com/dp/B0FS5VD2GL

Shalom!

Table of Contents

Introduction: Meditating through the Bible	1
1. The Evening Time Meditation	10
2. Live in the Now Moment	16
3. Celebratory Meditation	26
4. Value Meditation, Not Diminish It	30
5. Meditate Whether Day or Night	36
6. Nations Meditate. Why Don't You Meditate?	42
7. Does God Consider Your Meditation?	50
8. Psalm with Silence Embedded In It	56
9. Is Your Meditation One from the Heart?	66
10. Where Do You Dwell at All Times?	72
11. Against the Meditators of Treachery	82
12. Wisdom, Understanding, & the Heart	88
13. Night Watches and Meditating on God	94
14. Meditation and That Song in the Night	100
15. Believe the Works of God Meditation	106
16. Your Meditation Can Be Sweet to God	114
17. Spell It Out Meditation	120
18. My Identity Meditation	126
19. Stillness Meditation	136

20. Trust Meditation	144
21. Communion & Remembrance Meditation	152
22. Fall in Love with Precept Meditation	160
23. Meditation on God's Testimonies	166
24. The Secrets of Enoch's Walk with God	172
25. Be Careful of Meditation on Fear	180
26. Whatsoever Virtuous Things Meditation	186
27. The Lord's Prayer and Your Needs	190
28. Is the Bush Burning? -A Meditation	204
29. Meditate upon Your Dreams and Visions	216
30. The Duties of Your Calling Meditation	224
31. Knowledge, Wisdom, Understanding & Meditation in Life	228

Introduction

MEDITATING THROUGH THE BIBLE

Rediscover the Powerful Perspective to Life

∞

The art of meditation is as ancient as human history and as modern as contemporary thought.

The origin of the word meditation should not be confused with the practice thereof. In an age where information is at our fingertips, it is easy to search and gain an understanding of how certain words we use today have evolved with the development of languages from before the demise of the Tower of Babel or even the antediluvian world.

The Word Meditation:

The word "meditation" comes from the Latin "meditatum", the past participle of "meditari", meaning to think deeply, reflect, or contemplate. The root word "med" implies taking appropriate measures.

From the definition of meditation, it is clear that meditation can be achieved in quiet, expressive, or interactive processes whenever the thought process is involved. Meditation is an invisible act of taking essential measures during contemplation or deep thought.

Notice that meditation by itself does not stop evil and pervasive thoughts and neither does it hinder good and worthy reflections. It is a process by which we can sharpen our intent whether good or bad.

MEDITATING THROUGH THE BIBLE

The Hebrew Bible Meditation:

In the Hebrew Bible, "Hagah" (or "haga") is the word for meditation. It first appears when God instructs Joshua to meditate on the law given to the children of Israel day and night for success and prosperity.

To Joshua, a man no nation could ever withstand and win a war against, meditation was God's prescription for success and a prosperous destiny.

> The Lord has made Himself known; He executes judgment; the wicked are snared in the work of their own hands. Higgaion [meditation]. Selah [pause, and calmly think of that]!
>
> ∞ Psalm 9:16 AMPC ∞

"Selah" is a word many scholars think is related to meditation, but its meaning and origin are unknown. It is mentioned over 50 times in the Psalm alone at the end of some verses. Because of its placement at the end of a verse, some deduct by reason that it is a liturgical or musical notation giving direction to the reader to pause, meditate, consider, and praise and worship God for His goodness.

"Higgaion" is one mysterious word that appears in the Psalm, between the lines, as it were. Early Bible scholars debated its meaning, and the modern ones do as well. Insights into the relevance of this word will be covered in chapter 8 of this book.

INTRODUCTION

The Definition of Meditation:

In this modern age, the word meditate is considered to mean the following:

> Meditation
> 1. to focus one's thoughts on: reflect on or ponder.
> 2. to plan or project in the mind: intend, purpose.
>
> **Merriam-Webster Dictionary**

Here is another dictionary's definition of the same word:

> 1. think deeply or focus one's mind for some time, in silence or with the aid of chanting, for religious or spiritual purposes, or as a method of relaxation.
> 2. think deeply or carefully about (something).
>
> **Oxford Dictionary**

Since meditation is associated with the act of thinking or measuring thoughts, imagination, or intentions, it is without reason that anytime we have had thoughts or reflections, whether they are deep or superficial, whether on God, ourselves, or on things, we have meditated.

The coming chapters of this book pull different Bible verses that show and outline God's plans and intentions for humanity. Conversely, we can also discover how our plans and intentions, and interacting with God's plan and purpose, can influence our destinies.

From Isaac to Jesus

Having laid the basis of the history of meditation, and its meaning, careful research will show that Isaac was meditating as he walked and prayed in the field. This was in the 20th-19th Century BCE. Yet words directly mentioning meditation would not appear in verified texts till about the 15th century BCE and more prevalently by the 10th Century BCE.

In the Bible, it is evident that Jesus practiced meditation, but this depends on understanding the context of what He was doing. Jesus spent much time in solitary prayer and contemplation. For instance, Luke 5:16 states that Jesus often withdrew to lonely and quiet places to pray. He not only did this, but He encouraged His disciples to do this as well.

> Then Jesus said, "Let's go off by ourselves to a quiet place and rest awhile." He said this because there were so many people coming and going that Jesus and his apostles didn't even have time to eat. So, they left by boat for a quiet place, where they could be alone.
>
> ∞ Mark 6:31-32 NLT ∞

From Yeshua's 40-day fast, His temptation, and His victory against Satan to His cry at the cross, you can perceive the meditation moments He engaged in. The lack of explicit mention of this word does not negate the clear and glaring evidence of the practice of meditation by Jesus, the Christ.

INTRODUCTION

One of the hallmarks of Jesus' ministering moments was teaching by parables to the masses of people. When He was alone with the disciples, Jesus would expound on His previous parable-based teaching. Notice how He talks about knowledge, wisdom, and revelation given to the steadfast disciple but not given to the come-and-go crowd:

> He answered and said unto them, "Because it is given unto you to know the mysteries of the kingdom of heaven, but to them, it is not given".
>
> ∞ Matthew 13:11 KJV ∞

As you will begin to understand with each Bible verse this book expounds on regarding meditation, you can never separate praise, worship, knowledge, wisdom, and meditation from who God is. Humanity can effectively approach Him through these practices. The most successful people come to be by embracing and practicing these principles.

Christian Bible Meditation and Other Practices:

I do not seek to highlight, undermine, or advance other meditation practices with the publication of this book. This book focuses on Biblical meditation practices. In this book, I am simply laying out what has inspired me, pulling it from the sacred writings of the Holy Bible to show the Biblical instances of meditation, and how I have come to practice Biblically based meditations.

I have not practiced other religious forms of meditation than those based in the Christian faith Bible and therefore cannot comment on them.

Whether you are coming before the presence of God in quietness, without thought, and waiting on Him or your approach is filled with thoughts and words to strike a deal, you are before Him. Whether God answers your thoughtless quietness or your forever-in-thought contemplation, no one can dispute what you are doing.

Our most important decisions and turning points are defined from the moments we stop and in the quietness of emotions separate the glitter from the real gold. As for what may be acceptable and what is permissible but has no fruitfulness, you are on the road to discovering it if you meditate.

We Are Part of God's Thoughts

Lastly, in this introduction, let me go on a journey with you to before the foundations of the universe. Let's go back to when all we can see and cannot see was not there and the Eternal Being existed alone.

How did He write our names in the Lamb's Book of Life (Revelation 21:27)?

With no physical or unseen matter yet created, how could that book exist? Can you see how we are part of God's eternal meditations?

Before we entered this sphere of existence were we not a part of His thoughts? If so, do we then have an eternal existence because of all this?

We are embedded in the thoughts of His heart through time and eternity.

In the book of Proverbs Chapter 8, wisdom was speaking out in this manner:

INTRODUCTION

> The Lord formed and brought me [Wisdom] forth at the beginning of His way, before His acts of old. I [Wisdom] was inaugurated and ordained from everlasting, from the beginning, before ever the earth existed.
>
> ∞ Proverbs 8:22-23 AMPC ∞

And wisdom continues to elaborate its interaction with the sons of men (though no man was yet created):

> Then I [Wisdom] was beside Him as a master and director of the work; and I was daily His delight, rejoicing before Him always. Rejoicing in His inhabited earth and delighting in the sons of men.
>
> ∞ Proverbs 8:30-31 AMPC ∞

Wisdom found it interesting to tether itself to the children of God, then and even now. Does this not excite you? We are created beings who once were and currently continue to be a series of thoughts by the Greatest One. We are founded and created from the Fountain of His Light (knowledge, wisdom, and revelation) through His meditation (intention, purpose). If God envisioned us before He created us, I am glad and will not doubt that it is through His meditation and creative power that I am here. What about you?

MEDITATING THROUGH THE BIBLE

Supernally Inspired Meditation Encounters.

Enjoy your journey through this book. May you experience supernal, inspired meditation moments and encounters. Here are a few keys to unlocking your encounters with God:

- Seek His Person and Heart more than you seek the advantage of you associating with Him. You cannot fool Him.

- Be honest. He already knows who you are.

- If there was no more grace and mercy for you, you would not be here. Let alone reading this book. Circumstances and the past do not define you. They teach all of us. Pass the past and embrace the now moment.

Just based on the definition of meditation, can you see how often you may have meditated unaware?

Arise! Let us go into this book.

Chapter 1

THE EVENING TIME MEDITATION

> And Isaac went out to meditate and bow down [in prayer] in the open country in the evening; and he looked up and saw that, behold, the camels were coming.
>
> ∞ Genesis 24:63 AMPC ∞

This is one of my favorite scriptures in the Pentateuch. It's not just the beauty of the story, but the deep teachings of God embedded in it that bring me joy. This is the first scripture that mentions meditation. How Isaac meditated, why, and from whom he learned it is not recorded.

I will illustrate this scripture here as follows:

Isaac was filled with anticipation. Eliezer's success on his mission was still unknown. There was no word back to Abraham and Isaac about his journey. As evening shadows fell, Isaac's meditation in the open field was interrupted by the sound of camels' hooves in the distance. From the path the camels took, passing by the well at Beer Lahairoi, Isaac deduced they were headed towards his homestead.

Rebekah, traveling from the city of Nahor, was finishing freshening up. Eliezer had informed her they had entered the outskirts of Beersheba, where his master lived. Rebekah opened the curtain of her carriage to look outside and smell the fresh scent of the field flowers. She saw a man standing at the other end of the field and asked Eliezer about him.

At that moment, Isaac lifted his eyes and looked towards the road to Mesopotamia. Shielding his eyes with his hand, he peered through the streaks of evening light. It was his camels. Eliezer was back! On one of the camels sat a colorfully dressed figure in a palanquin-like saddle. Isaac's heart raced, and he ran across the field to meet the camel train.

A woman, blessed with the mandate that her descendants would possess the gates of their enemies, had arrived at Beer Lahairoi. Eliezer pointed to the man in the field and told Rebekah, "Madam, behold, your bridegroom cometh!" She had asked him about the man's identity. Rebekah dismounted the camel, took a veil, and covered herself. To this day, brides still choose to cover themselves with a veil on their wedding day.

I do not know exactly how she got to the homestead from here, but this last part is an easy contemplation for you if you indulge it.

If you wonder how and in what ways Isaac meditated to have such beautiful outcomes, you are not alone.

The first mention of meditation in the Bible is an evening time meditation. Isaac was in the field meditating. This is significant. Could it be that people before him also meditated? Here are a few other evening time fellowships with God that likely included meditation, even if not explicitly mentioned:

Adam & Eve

Adam fellowshipped with God during sunset. At the evening time God came calling to Adam. Even after Adam and Eve had sinned and were hiding, God's voice still compelled them to respond rather than remain silent. There is something about His Voice. All creation responds when He speaks to it. He cannot be ignored. To Adam and Eve, He would come walking and they heard the sound of His approach at the evening time.

THE EVENING TIME MEDITATION

Abraham

Abraham laid a heifer, a goat, a ram, a turtledove, and a young pigeon as sacrifices and watched over them as the sun set. His encounter with God continued from sunset until nighttime. It was quite dark outside when God moved in between the carcasses and spoke to Him. His children knew of Egyptian slavery coming before it did.

Jacob

Jacob gathered stones from a broken altar at Luz for a pillow when the sun was setting on him. He had a fabulous visitation from God in a dream that changed his life and outlook forever. Talk about an evening time choice of a place for a runaway to lie down for the night!

Elijah

How did the prophet Elijah know that fire will only come down on the wet and drenched sacrifice he will make and none on the prophets of Baal and Asherah?

At evening time, God always shows up. May the meditation of your heart and your sacrifice be acceptable before Him. There are simply no antics required with God if you want to see His fire fall over your evening sacrifice. Before you build your altar for sacrifice, cultivate your capacity to hear God's instructions by meditation.

The significance of evening-time meditation and worship is that it reminds us God has never abandoned fellowship with us since Adam. Most people find it hard to believe this as their evening time is clouded by work, commute, and fellowship with friends.

It is not that God is not available to us but that like Adam we are hiding behind our routines as Adam did behind the bushes with leaf aprons covering him.

If you find praise, worship, and meditation laborious, overhaul your approach. Angels in heaven do it, continuously, eternally, not out of duty but because they are in awe of God. Do it because you know and believe God is awesome.

The times of meditation extending beyond sunset are referred to as the night watches. Read more about the night watches in Chapter 13 of this book as we uncover King David's approach to nighttime.

The Significance of the Evening Time Meditation

Let me introduce you to the profound concepts surrounding evening meditation, as revealed through the story of Isaac in Scripture. The Holy Spirit of God, when dwelling within us, teaches us to think deeply, be relevant, and reflect in contemplation. Whether you are on the go or seated cross-legged, make it a point to engage in meditation. Notice that this practice is most effective when we are yielded vessels to Him. Here are some key points to consider:

- **Thanksgiving:** Evening meditation is a time to reflect on and give thanks to God for the day.

- **Possibilities and Freshness:** Meditating in an open field symbolizes standing in the realm of endless possibilities and renewal, regardless of how your day went.

THE EVENING TIME MEDITATION

- **Expectation:** After meditation, lift your head and look forward with expectation to what you desire.

- **Fellowship with God:** This practice is akin to the cool-of-the-day fellowship that Adam and Eve experienced in the Garden of Eden. Identify with Isaac's evening time practice of meditation.

- **Purposeful Solitude:** It is a God-centered, intentional solitude.

- **Attuned Listening:** Evening time meditation tunes your ear to the sounds coming from the road of expectations.

- **Refreshment:** End your day refreshed by the waters from the Living One, just as Isaac was quenched by the well at Beer Lahairoi, "the God who sees me."

- **Destiny and Success:** Meditation brings you into alignment with your destiny, good news, and success. Good things

- **Gratitude and Humility:** Learn to cloak yourself in gratitude to God when your journey is successful, and you are satisfied with His direction.

By incorporating these elements into your evening meditation (appropriate good intentional contemplation), you can deepen your spiritual practice and enhance your connection with God.

Chapter 2

∞

LIVE IN THE NOW MOMENT

> This Book of the Law shall not depart out of your mouth, but you shall meditate on it day and night, that you may observe and do according to all that is written in it. For then you shall make your way prosperous, and then you shall deal wisely and have 'good' success.
>
> ∞ Joshua 1:8 AMPC ∞

Confidently Live in the NOW MOMENT

Every time I read or listen to the book of Joshua, I check myself to see if I am confidently living in the "now moment". Living in the "now moment" means realizing and actively believing that now is the time when God is favoring you. Do not hesitate to step into His favor.

> NOW, after the death of His servant Moses, the LORD spoke to Joshua, son of Nun, Moses' assistant, saying, ...
>
> ∞ Joshua 1:1 BSB ∞

God is not looking at your loss and lost on what to do next. God is not in a bereavement period at any one time. There is no record of a vision of God sitting down and counting His losses. All things come back in full circle to Him, having accomplished what He intended and what pleases HIM. Just refuse to let your life end a loss.

Notice God appointed none else but Himself to reposition Joshua. In the 'now' moment, it just takes a word or thought from Him, and you will be set.

MEDITATING THROUGH THE BIBLE

> The centurion answered, "Lord, I am not worthy to have You come under my roof. But just say the word, and my servant will be healed. For I myself am a man under authority, with soldiers under me. I tell one to go, and he goes; and another to come, and he comes. I tell my servant to do something, and he does it."
>
> ∞ Matthew 8:8-9 BSB ∞

Notice that we are not talking about just meditating on the verse that speaks directly to the art of meditation. God enthusiastically mentions the Book of the Law. He bids us to meditate day and night therein as a prescription for "good" success and prosperous endeavors.

Meditation here is more than immersing oneself in the letter and the intent of the precept.

Allow yourself to traverse into the mind and intentions of God as you enter and live in this realm by meditating on His words. To do this effectively, your heart must be into God's nature and your spirit will automatically seek diligently to know and avail God's life and wisdom to you.

Success collides with those who abide in the now moment. Success is a stranger to the one living in their past while looking to the future.

A freedom fighter who has fought in the war and won many battles does not seek to relive the ordeals of the warzone. They want to live freely in the hard-won freedom some of their fellow soldiers may have died to secure.

Most people will clutch onto the first excuse to justify and feel comforted when faced with failure or loss in their endeavors. Yet we claim to be the keepers of an unfailing God's covenant. "A fool that utters all his unwise counsel" like a burst pipe is what we have been reduced to most times.

LIVE IN THE NOW MOMENT

Losing more by spouting out at the wrong point what should be contained and channeled to purpose at the correct juncture.

We no longer see the power of an invincible God manifesting through the majority of believers—even among those considered eminent. Instead, we default to reactive prayers for those struck by calamity. Yet the afflicted already know—whether spoken or not—that these prayers often ring hollow: faithless, lacking empathy, and void of restorative power, because they do not truly please God. Why delay taking preventive measures against life threatening excesses and only stand to pray when precious lives are lost?

We have failed—not only in our direct actions but also in our silence and passive bystanding. And when we excuse our lack of zeal and divine power with a resigned "What else can we do?" we risk reducing God and prayer to mere instruments of political, economic, or religious grandstanding.

But there is a better way. No matter how small your voice, your helping hand, or your capacity to create change—start with that. Do not despise what you hold in your hand, your mind, or your spirit. Act now, in the present moment. Make your words, your actions, and your presence count.

Those who truly know their God—not by hearsay, but through personal experience—are the ones who accomplish great exploits. They take conscious, intentional steps.

So, rise. Stand up. Be counted among those who pursue the highest good—for the people and for God.

We clearly read that God spoke to Moses. But we also clearly read that God spoke to Joshua pertaining to the things happening in his day and time after Moses had died. God is not just a God of yesterday, but he is the God of today and tomorrow as well.

MEDITATING THROUGH THE BIBLE

> Jesus Christ (the Messiah) is [always] the same, yesterday, today, [yes] and forever (to the ages).
>
> ∞ Hebrews 13:8 AMPC ∞

Joshua's Meditation

In what ways did Joshua meditate to live such an undefeated life? How many excuses did he lodge before God against God's promises?

If we have fallen into a ditch because we closed our eyes to the reality before us, why try to point fingers at the nearest disliked bystander? Let's meditate before we step. There is no need to stoop low. The meditation of a diligent person will manifest God's way out and how one's steps are to be ordered.

King David wrote in Psalm 40:6-8 that "sacrifice and offering" was not what God desired but a prepared body that He could pour the volume of the book into to make it a living epistle.

Reflect on your life. What does the life-written record of your life read like? Are there failures, disappointments, and defeats that stretch the tapestry of your existence to the extent that your living record seems like a record of the dead while alive?

This kind of life, though troubled, can be turned around. It should start with your realization that you need God, the volume of the book, and meditation but not Moses, just like Joshua. The now moment is not centered on any man or prophet. Train your thoughts to stay on God, the precept, and the present.

Let's draw lessons from three distinct encounters between God and his children. Familiarize with Moses by the burning bush, with God speaking

LIVE IN THE NOW MOMENT

to Joshua and seeing the captain of the LORD's host, and with God speaking after Jesus Christ is transfigured.

Seek to understand the "now moment" actions that arise from these encounters:

1. **Arise and Act:** Do not just train your mind but arise. Lift yourself and begin walking towards God's promises. Most believers' problem is that they stay too long on the same mountain (achievement, recognition, plateau).

2. **Possess your inheritance:** Go on to possess what God has given you. The mountain you hear God's voice on is not a place for you to stay but one to be energized at for the possession ahead. Do not be caught up in the building of tabernacles for God's servants on top of this mountain.

3. **Deliver and Position Others:** There are people to deliver from afflictions, to position in their destinies, and to unleash to do greater works. There is work to be done. You cannot stay in the same routine because the Voice bids you to go.

4. **Hear God Directly:** Hear from God directly and not just through God's servants. God's voice from the top of the mountain said, "This is my beloved Son in whom I am well pleased to dwell. Hear Him". If the Holy Spirit of God dwells within you, hear Him from within you.

5. **You Are the One to Do It:** You are God's general to divide the inheritance in your family. The angels of God, like the captain of the LORD's hosts, fight on your behalf as long as you engage in possessing what is given to you.

MEDITATING THROUGH THE BIBLE

We do not see visibly the Captain of the LORD's host armies when Joshua stepped out to fight and possess the land promised to Israel. Neither do we see Moses and Elijah after the transfiguration. But we see Jesus only to the crucifixion and after ascension.

Beyond looking at Jesus who was taken up into heaven, look at yourself. All that Jesus is was poured into the body of Christ, of which you are part of. Jesus said even the Father and Him will come and make their abode with us. We know this and must exercise confidence that we have become the habitation "in whom God is well pleased to dwell".

And all who say they hear God should also hear Him through us. God has not taken or chosen to side with one group of people more than the other. He is with those who have received Him. We should not outsource hearing from God to others. That has never been God's intent. Otherwise, Christ's death is in vain.

> His purpose was that now, through the church, the manifold wisdom of God should be made known to the rulers and authorities in the heavenly realms, according to the eternal purpose that He accomplished in Christ Jesus our Lord. In Him and through faith in Him we may enter God's presence with boldness and confidence.
>
> ∞ Ephesians 3:10-12 BSB ∞

This is the essence of living in the 'now moment'. It's like having eternity embedded in human flesh and letting the human flesh be subject to celestial order.

LIVE IN THE NOW MOMENT

Living in the NOW Moment Meditation Guide

- **Past vs. Present:** What has been is not what is and will be to the one who refuses being enslaved to vanity, mediocrity, and unrighteous patterns. You are not your past experiences, failures, successes, or imaginations. You are an eternal spirit having an earthly experience. Look at yourself beyond the limitations and pain of the earthen vessel you are housed in. Why resign to a fate that is based on the past or lineage you had no control over and chose to toss the opportunity to chart your own in the present?

- **Rely on Your Now Identity:** Trust in yourself (where God is) and in God who is present with you. Know God is in you. Let God sit on the throne of (rule) your spirit.

- **Seek Better Partnerships:** No human being, pastor, prophet, teacher, business, parent, spouse, country, or government has ever made (created) you. They are here only to help you, if they can help. Seek better partnerships with all of these where applicable.

- **Reflect on the Past Briefly:** Have short and precise reflections (meditation) on the past to know what to not do, what to do better, who to leave behind in the past, and what to take with you into now and the future. But do not dwell in the past. All that is in the past lasted until then but not now.

- **Reduce Stress:** Remove stress and distress by focusing your energies on now.

- **Be Present:** The now moment is an omnipresent time. God lives in eternity where the past and the future are both swallowed by the present.

MEDITATING THROUGH THE BIBLE

- **Act Now:** Do what you can do now. Rise up and do it now. Relocate your body and mind by letting go, reaching, and attaching to the present good and the future.

- **Think Positively:** Think good now. Tune out negative voices now.

- **Worship And Praise:** Worship better now than then. Praise God better now than then.

- **Speak Up:** Communicate better now than then.

- **See Success:** Refuse to see failure which is defined by what has been but the now moment, being present and the future only hold what you can do better.

- **Set Goals:** Take steps to ensure success. Set achievable goals for now and the future.

- **Hear God and Hear Good:** Hear the present. Pay attention to the now-moment voice inside of you. Hear God now.

Living in the now moment is more than living beyond your past God encounters and beyond your past good memories. See yourself in the glorious atmosphere of the Omnipresent One. God is a God of the now moment.

While we are here, let me point you to who you are. Who are you? You are your "I am …". You are not your "I was …" or yet your "I will …". In the same manner, God is not defined by the past or the future but by His present. This is why He is eternal. Eternal does not denote the absence of time but that time, both the past, present, and the future, is swallowed up by His consistency and timeless nature.

Meditate on the Word of God while contemplating the following poem:

LIVE IN THE NOW MOMENT

MY I AM IS

My I am is not my past and failures
My I am is not my pain and fears
My I am is more than what I feel
My I am is more than I can imagine

I am in the image of Elohim,
A ben-Elohim (child of Elohim)
I am part of His substance
I am His voice in the now
I am part of His omnipresent revelation

Omnipotent God and Father
Here I am, I am Yours
Worshipping and praising You
I look at You, living in me

My I am believes and never doubts
My I am worships and praises my God
My I am succeeds and prospers
My I am lives in the now moment

Chapter 3

CELEBRATORY MEDITATION

∞

> Sing to Him, sing praises to Him; meditate on and talk of all His wondrous works and devoutly praise them!
>
> ∞ 1 Chronicles 16:9 AMPC ∞

Are you celebrating a recent success? Reflect on it and praise God. Celebrate God in meditation. Do you have a past victory that continues to inspire you? Celebrate and praise God who fights your battles.

Esau, robbed of the blessing by Jacob, cried and wrestled a blessing out of his father.

> Esau said to his father, Have you only one blessing, my father? Bless me, even me also, O my father! And Esau lifted up [could not control] his voice and wept aloud. Then Isaac his father answered, Your [blessing and] dwelling shall all come from the fruitfulness of the earth and from the dew of the heavens above;
>
> ∞ Genesis 27:38-39 AMPC ∞

In his life, Esau was not blessed any less than the affluent of our time nor are his descendants destitute. *If God can so bless a man that He says, "Esau, I hated", how much more can He bless us whom He loves?* If you cannot see His blessings on you yet, still celebrate God for who He is.

Esau's long, prosperous life shows that success and prosperity are not measures of righteousness but of diligence. Generational wealth often reflects God's favor more than individual righteousness. Esau was diligent in extracting whatever good was left in his father's pronunciation of a blessing. There is a record of the man's wealth despite his estrangement with God.

Recognize God's Wondrous Works

It is not true that we cannot find God's wondrous works. We just need to blink and see what is in front of us and testify to it. Yet, indeed, God's works do not hold a devoutly praised significance in humans. We choose to be willfully spiritually ignorant. Our own "good" works we praise while exfoliating the heavens at the slightest excuse we envisage.

Praising good works is important. It starts with being good at praising others. Commending others for achieving good things is not an easy thing especially if you have not done it before. The fact that it feels awkward to do so tells you that it is most important and rewarding to you who must commend others. When you find it difficult to do a good thing, though simple it may be, it means that a good thing has a good return value for you.

The Bible teaches us that if we cannot love our sister or brother whom we see, we cannot love God whom our eyes cannot behold. The simplest evidence of loving God is loving our brothers and sisters. If you love, you celebrate what you love.

Meditate While You Celebrate!

- **Praise In All Circumstances:** You may not have anything to your name. You may not have great possessions. You may be the poorest of the poor but do not be robbed of the capacity to praise good

CELEBRATORY MEDITATION

works when you can. From this, you can build up and praise God for everything.

- **Acknowledge Others:** By praising good works, you praise God who created mankind. God has given humankind great and beautiful minds to create and invent wonderful things.

- **Reflect on Nature:** Go out to nature and see the beauty that surpasses all. You will understand how walking past mountain ranges, navigating a creek in the valley, and looking up from the top of the mountain is worth praising God for. An act as simple as sitting down to watch the sunset or to view the rising of the sun is such a wonderful experience. It is a moment worth praising God for. You have not commanded the sun to set or to rise. God has commanded it for our benefit.

- **Appreciate Creation's Creations:** Have you seen the birds flying, perched on hidden branches, foraging for food, making the sound of myriad voices that make such a beautiful symphony? Do you see or understand if they worry like you do?

- **Focus on Solutions:** Are you hungry? Focus not on the hunger but praise God and look around you. When you lift from meditation without worry you will see that there is a pathway of solutions that waits for your direction.

Living in the now moment involves recognizing and celebrating God's works around us. It means praising Him in all circumstances and meditating on His goodness. By doing so, we align ourselves with His eternal presence and experience His blessings in our lives.

Chapter 4

VALUE MEDITATION, NOT DIMINISH IT

> Indeed, you are doing away with [reverential] fear, and you are hindering and diminishing meditation and devotion before God.
>
> ∞ Job 15:4 AMPC ∞

The above verse is the record of an accusation leveled at Job by Eliphaz the Temanite, a "physician" and friend of Job who came to "console" him and sit by the ash heap with him.

If this statement were what Job was doing, would it have justified the loss of his family and the sores so deep in his body that they could see the white bone? Job's friends were out by the ash dump not to wash his putrefied sores or medicate or bind them with love and support. They came to examine him for secret sins. They came to draw out a narrative that God was judging him. To them, he was an insolent prideful man railing against God for a judgement he well deserved.

We have these kinds of friends sometimes.

Because sometimes calamities happen to us to correct our waywardness and bring us back on track, it does not mean that when we see calamity on any one of us, we should extrapolate it to sin or punishment for sin.

God knew Job. God had total confidence in Job. His friends believed in God. But that was not a license for them to wear the rights of a judge. They wrongly used the scales of justice on behalf of God to condemn a man that God knew and boasted of to the devil.

God bragged about Job. That is why God allowed calamity to pass by Job's dwelling.

MEDITATING THROUGH THE BIBLE

The devil had not managed to lay a finger on Job all the times he had tried. Satan shifted his plan to make conjectures on Job's reaction to substantial loss as a trigger that can get Job to curse God. It seems trivial to think that Satan suspended his to-and-fro globe-trotting to come before God's presence and then hear Adonai boast about a man. Satan then proceeded to ask God for permission to sift Job, a man. Does something seem baffling here?

What exactly did Satan come before God for? It was not because he saw God's people in a predicament and wanted to implore God on their behalf. Could it be that Satan saw one man upon the earth who had not cursed God to His face, and he was not happy about that?

If Satan had an audience with God, how come someone wants to believe God does not want to hear them? Why does the devil get to manage to be in the presence of God and you cannot seem to do that yourself?

If the devil asks God concerning us for a similar sifting, what would be our outcome?

Faith stands taller than any challenge or predicament if we can use it. It is a victory that we already have.

It is true if you do away with the fear of God, you will diminish God's worship. You may still meditate. However, you will have canceled the capacity to have a positive relationship with the Creator. In this case, you will not be different from Satan himself who desecrated the sanctity of recognizing God as the only one who should be worshiped.

This is why worship and meditation are important to be practiced in the context of the respect and worship of the Creator more than it is for any other entity, intent, or purpose.

An example that comes to mind is Cain who was angry with his brother Abel for something that Abel was not responsible for. Abel was not

VALUE MEDITATION, NOT DIMINISH IT

responsible for God rejecting Cain's sacrifice. The reason for Cain's sacrifice not being accepted by God was Cain's lack of knowledge, wisdom, understanding, meditation, worship, and sacrificing intention inspired by revelation.

You see, revelation is a product of faith. Faith is an intention to trust and rely on the one you have it (the faith) in. Faith is not a fear or a feeling of dependence. Faith does not evaporate in the presence of calamity, nor does it disappear when there is no need for dependence.

A great example is a child holding a parent's hand. In an exceedingly difficult situation, they may be afraid of what is coming at them but because of faith in the parent, they hold on to that hand, not running away but facing the challenge head-on.

We have a Father who is bigger than our problems and challenges. He holds us in his hand, and we need not fear anything. Though we may close our eyes when calamity is coming towards us, we should not let go of that hand and run on our own.

Every storm loses its power before His feet. So, keep on holding to God's unchanging hand.

A Meditation Based on Job

1. **Place Yourself In Job's Shoes:** Reflect on your life before, during, and after a calamity.

    a. What do you see about yourself?

    b. Can God trust you with the same confidence as he had concerning Job? Why or why not?

2. **God's Confidence In Us:** Far from a negative answer to the preceding question, God always has confidence in us. We just don't always have it about ourselves. We end up drinking baby milk not because we deserve to be treated like babies but because we fear.

3. **Keep Your Flesh Silent To Hear God:** Job learned that great swelling words and well-crafted arguments do not move God. Nor do they stop your detractors from fighting you when you are already down. Faith believes and relies on God to guide it into the how. The faster you silence your flesh the better you can hear God and be free.

4. **Read Between The Lines:** Look for God's plan in your calamities on how to overcome. Do not condemn yourself, drawback, or quit. Integrally stand positive that God is good and believe there is a way out. You will see God's guiding hand out of the situation.

5. **Go To God When In A Calamity:** The devil came before the presence of God, but it seems that Job, in his sorrow and upon the ash heap, could not. Look at your circumstances and change your approach to God.

6. **Approach God With Faith:** Approaching God does not require faith but receiving something from God does. Do not be defeated by the devil's request, in his faith, to sift you. Believe in God, in your faith, to bless and more than sustain you.

Value meditation and reverence for God. They are essential for a strong relationship with the Creator. In times of trouble, hold on to your faith and trust in God's plan. Meditate and reflect on Job's story and find strength in knowing that God has confidence in you.

Chapter 5

MEDITATE WHETHER DAY OR NIGHT

> But his delight is in the law of the LORD; and in his law doth he meditates day and night.
>
> ∞ Psalm 1:2 KJV ∞

Psalm Chapter 1 is one of the most interesting scriptures in the Bible. It gives a blueprint of the blessed individual. If you are looking to live a life that is blessed, pay attention to meditate on Psalm Chapter 1. No holy Scripture gives a better prescription for a blessed individual than Psalm Chapter 1.

The key to being a blessed person is an immense delight in the law of the Lord. If you delight in God's precepts so much that your life becomes a tapestry of them, your life will reflect the words of God. Most people, when understanding the law, take advantage of it to break it for gain. However, if your day and night are filled with meditation and gladness to follow the law of the Lord, there is no room to corrupt yourself by the same law.

Ever wondered why God told Joshua to meditate on the book of the law day and night? God was teaching Joshua to live and meditate in the present. I have seen people who have prayed day and night without ceasing and yet have not received answers to their prayers. I cannot say the same about those who have meditated on the law of the Lord, day and night. Joshua's undefeated life is the first evidence of how meditation is a key to success and prosperity.

At some point in the history of the scriptures, meditation was overshadowed by prayer. While true prayer is a request, meditation is a reflection and deep cognitive intention on the Divine. These two, prayer and meditation, should coexist just like faith and belief do. The law of the Lord mentioned here is not to punish wrong and right but more so to reveal the principles of how a spiritual God operates in the physical and spiritual realms. It informs our spirit to be like Him and to have dominion upon the Earth.

I can show you devout people who have followed the dos and don'ts of the law and yet are poor, miserable, wretched, and live without hope. The Scripture records that the letter of the law kills, but the Spirit gives life. There is the Spirit behind the law of the Lord. If you tap into the Spirit behind the principles of the Lord, you will be like Joshua for whom success and prosperity were companions.

The concept of day and night here is boundless in time. Remember Joshua in the battle against the Amorites prayed to God and told the sun to stand still upon Gibeon and the moon to give light in the valley of Aijalon until the battle was settled. He had to fight Sisera and win. Most of us, when the sun sets, want to give up and start the fight again when it is light. We do not think about stopping the sun from setting on us. But Joshua's meditation taught him to speak to the sun to shine beyond its set cycle of time.

Do you need to succeed in your mission? Harness your environment to work on your behalf. The problem with our faith is we believe there is only one sun and that we do not order its footsteps. We see one sun, but there is more than one light. Some are so invisible that it takes faith to walk in that light when all you see is pervasive darkness.

If we meditate regardless of the seasons of light and darkness, we are no longer subjects of the timelines of the momentary darkness and light cycle. When seasons do not control us, the reverse becomes the reality. We begin to create our own atmosphere, our own seasons, and our own environment. The elements of our new environment become malleable to our design and intent.

God is not subject to earthly seasons or time. He is eternal. Yesterday, today, and forever are not lost or beyond reach to Him. Was Job not restored? And double for his troubles! Notice, God required Job to pray for

MEDITATE WHETHER DAY OR NIGHT

his friends. God's wrath was kindled against Eliphaz and company because they made God look like a punisher of the righteous (Job in this instance). Eliphaz, Bildad, and Zophar brought sacrifices to Job for him to intercede on their behalf.

Despite Job's loss and accusations leveled at him, his restoration hinged on him showing mercy and grace to his frenemies.

> So Eliphaz the Temanite and Bildad the Shuhite and Zophar the Naamathite went and did according as the LORD commanded them: the LORD also accepted Job. And the LORD turned the captivity of Job, when he prayed for his friends: also, the LORD gave Job twice as much as he had before.
>
> ∞ Job 42:9-10 KJV ∞

What about Job's wife telling him he was better off cursing God and dying? (Job2:9) You do not hear of an instance where God was wroth with her. Some among us mistake their spouses for the devil when going through immense suffering, despair, and frustration. A husband and wife are ONE before God. No matter how diverse a husband and wife's earthly troubles or successes are, Jesus says in Matthew 19:5-6 AMPC, *"... and the two shall become one flesh? So, they are no longer two, but one flesh. What therefore God has joined together, let not man put asunder (separate)."*

Even if they squabbled, do not think for a moment that Job's wife really wanted him to curse God and be eternally lost. I bet you she was letting off steam. If Job forgave her and understood her, who are we to extrapolate? FYI, God did not do it either. There is no record of it.

If you find yourself second-guessing God based on your analysis of a situation and want to express personal opinions, remember your darkest moments are not hopeless before Him. Force yourself to lean on His unchanging nature. Before Him, nothing is lost. Nothing is dead before God except what has gone through the lake of fire.

Meditate whether it is day or night. If you want to see a new you, believe and thank God for it. Though the worms ate at Job's flesh away, he still believed he would see God in his flesh. This was a faith of proportions more than those of mere belief, understanding, and conviction.

> And the sea gave up the dead which were in it; and death and hell delivered up the dead which were in them: and they were judged every man according to their works
>
> ∞ Revelation 20:13 KJV ∞

A faith that transcends mere belief, knowledge, understanding, and conviction is an intensely alive and deeply profound faith. The earth and the sea know to give up the dead in them when God beckons. Job's faith gave him knowledge with a profound conviction that his earth, his flesh, and his eyes would not be eaten away by decay. He foresaw himself standing before God.

The Blessed Person's Meditation

Truly, you can be like a tree planted by the rivers of Living Waters whose life and fruit do not fail in any season. Failure and unfruitfulness are things

MEDITATE WHETHER DAY OR NIGHT

that meditation beyond day and night automatically remove from one's atmosphere. The counsel of the wicked can easily be seen and avoided. You cannot sit in the seat of the scornful when you are in the now moment. You will not hinder sinners from obtaining mercy before God.

> Blessed is the man who walks not in the counsel of the wicked, nor stands in the way of sinners, nor sits in the seat of scoffers; but his delight is in the law of the LORD, and on his law, he meditates day and night. He is like a tree planted by streams of water that yields its fruit in its season, and its leaf does not wither. In all that he does, he prospers.
>
> The wicked are not so, but are like chaff that the wind drives away. Therefore, the wicked will not stand in the judgment, nor sinners in the congregation of the righteous; for the LORD knows the way of the righteous, but the way of the wicked will perish.
>
> ∞ Psalm 1:1-6 ESV ∞

You do not live life competing with the person next door because you know where your strength comes from. By meditating and delighting in God's precepts, you have made a surety that all you do prospers. You do not have instability like the wicked who get blown away by winds like chaff.

Chapter 6

NATIONS MEDITATE. WHY DON'T YOU MEDITATE?

> WHY DO the nations assemble with commotion [uproar and confusion of voices], and why do the people imagine (meditate upon and devise) an empty scheme?
>
> ∞ Psalm 2:1 AMPC ∞

This scripture, though seldom taught, is profound and consequential.

Nations that seek to oppress you meditate on keeping you subservient. If it were not for God thwarting their plans, many of us would be in trouble. If malevolent individuals can meditate on draining your energy, what excuse do we have to not meditate ourselves?

We are called to meditate on God's principles, not to devise evil schemes but to counteract them.

David, the king, meditated and established a unique kingdom, winning many wars. He learned to protect his father's sheep from lions, teaching us that in diligently guarding the little we can be entrusted with more.

We are not to dwell on those who devise evil but to meditate on God's righteousness and wage war against self-defeating mindsets.

The King of Aram

The king of Aram thought that there was an enemy spy in the camp. He came to make war with Israel. Elisha the prophet, would tell the king of Israel the conversations and plans the king of Aram was making with his military generals. If you are against God's people, then even your thoughts and secret plans will be whispered into the ears of a man or woman of God.

MEDITATING THROUGH THE BIBLE

The choice is to be on the side of God and so in tune with Him. Without such a life we run the risk of our enemies planning against us while we feast at the same table with them. The table where we must be always found at is not our enemies' but the one that God who "preparest a table for me before my enemies" sets for us.

Take time to meditate concerning your environment. Prepare yourself against those who intend to do you harm. Your best defense is having the wisdom of God to the level where the walls, stones, and trees around your enemy listen on your behalf and tell you the secrets of what your enemy is planning.

> "I tell you," He replied, "if they keep quiet, the stones will cry out."
>
> ∞ Luke 19:40 NIV ∞

This is not a strange statement by the Lord. There is no element of substance upon the earth which does not obey God. It was the season for a witness to cry out "Hosannah, blessed is He who comes in the name of Adonai!". And if people muzzled their mouths, the stones were not going to remain verbally muted.

Remember Prophet Balaam was verbally rebuked by a donkey after it had tried all tricks to get him to pay attention. Talk about a seer not seeing what his ride was seeing! Sometimes, your whole atmosphere is spiritually charged with a singular assignment to the point that stones and water will do what is necessary to bring God's word to come to pass. In these situations, be found on the right side of God's intention.

NATIONS MEDITATE. WHY DON'T YOU MEDITATE?

The Shahanshah and "A King" under the Emperor

Haman sat at the Shahanshah's table and ate together with the Shah Ahasuerus (also known as Xerxes I) more than Queen Esther did. With a decree from the emperor making his subjects bow before Haman, what could go wrong for Haman? Haman pleased the king with how he helped the throne to govern. Haman's dreams deluded him to think that he was "a king" under the king. He had turned the whole national council of the king against the Jews. As if that was not enough, the people in his circle wanted the king dead.

> And he said unto the disciples, 'It is impossible for the stumbling blocks not to come, but woe [to him] through whom they come; it is more profitable to him if a weighty millstone is put round about his neck, and he hath been cast into the sea, than that he may cause one of these little ones to stumble
>
> ∞ Luke 17:1-2 YLT ∞

The man Mordecai was very insightful. He sat as an attendant in the corridors of power. Though Mordecai unraveled the assassination plot against the king, neither Haman nor the council made a request for the king to honor him.

Before Haman, all Jews had a secret guillotine awaiting them. To think and plan to wipe out an entire ethnic group was not something Haman feared. Haman oozed an offending and poisonous intention not only against Israel but against God and all humanity. Adolf Hitler and those who committed genocide would follow in his footsteps centuries later. All who walk in such ways sully the history of mankind.

Mordecai had respect for God enough to not bow to a man. It didn't matter that the king's directive was for the attendants to bow to Haman when he passed by.

If it were not for the insight of Mordecai, all the Jews would have perished at the hands of Haman. Mordecai observed his environment very well. He was able to read into and see the enemy's plots against the people of Israel.

Our level of respect for the personhood of leadership should never cloud our capacity to the extent of treating them like gods. Watch carefully the prideful ones who want to or lead and the ones who bootlick them. They commit treachery against mankind if they serve their image more than they serve the neediest in society.

> If you help the poor, you are lending to the LORD— and he will repay you!
>
> ∞ Proverbs 19:17 NLT ∞

The test for true leadership is in its capacity to answer the call to meet the needs of the people without enslaving them to the leader's power. In precise terms, we should not neglect the widow, the orphan, and the poor. We should not enslave them when working to meet their needs.

You are better off giving to the poor because in doing so, you are making God borrow from you. If you are a lending entity to God, what kind of return or profit can you envisage?

NATIONS MEDITATE. WHY DON'T YOU MEDITATE?

Dare to be a Daniel

A man was so attentive to Heaven, he had times of worship littered throughout his day. The term "meditation" is not explicitly used in the book of Daniel. Daniel's consistent prayer life and unwavering faith demonstrate a deep spiritual connection that informs of his meditative ways.

Daniel's regular practice of seeking God's presence and guidance aligns with the essence of meditation—focusing the mind, seeking inner peace, and connecting with the Divine One.

As for Daniel, the problem spanning the kingdom where he served atop the empire's leadership was a group of leaders who became jealous of this mighty man. Daniel had not lost his position of influence even though the kingdoms changed from the Babylonians to the Medes and the Persians after that.

Daniel's character was marked by integrity. He served various Babylonian and Medo-Persian kings with excellence and honesty.

Daniel 6:4-5 states that the officials could find no corruption in Daniel because he was trustworthy and diligent in his duties.

Being in that place where you know what your enemy is going to do and what God is going to do for you against your enemies' tactics is priceless. Who in the world would not want to be in such a place?

With Daniel, we see there is a way, even for a foreigner, to be so powerful that the leadership of a most powerful nation with renowned leaders cannot lead without his counsel. That way for Daniel was through knowledge, wisdom, understanding, meditation, worship, and prayer. He paid attention to the voice of God and to the pronouncements God had made concerning his people.

MEDITATING THROUGH THE BIBLE

> Forasmuch as an excellent spirit, and knowledge, and understanding, interpreting of dreams, and shewing of hard sentences, and dissolving of doubts, were found in the same Daniel, whom the king named Belteshazzar: now let Daniel be called, and he will shew the interpretation.
>
> ∞ Daniel 5:12 KJV ∞

Daniel was a man of an excellent spirit. Where can you find a spiritual and political man who can tell you in detail about the dream you have forgotten? And then proceed to tell you the meaning of it? And it happens exactly as he said in the course of history over many centuries.

The aspect where most of us miss it is not that we are men and women who pray or meditate as much today. We miss it by what we meditate or pray for. We miss it because of where our hearts rest or are inclined towards. If David, the king, never saw the righteous forsaken nor begging for bread, do we blame God for our lostness and drought?

We should allow not only our spirit and soul to be immersed in the knowledge, wisdom, and understanding of God. Building habits that fill our flesh (our earth) with His ways and taste invites Him to take center stage. If the earth shall be filled with the knowledge of His glory, why do you seek to resist His knowledge in your flesh? It is God's knowledge that reveals His magnificence.

> For the earth shall be filled with the knowledge of the glory of the LORD, as the waters cover the sea.
>
> ∞ Habakkuk 2:14 KJV ∞

Chapter 7

DOES GOD CONSIDER YOUR MEDITATION?

> Give ear to my words. O LORD, consider my meditation.
>
> ∞ Psalm 5:1 KJV ∞

Psalm 5 begins with the wonderful picture of a man pleading with God. He asks that God give ear to his words and consider the man's meditation. This man would cry in his meditation. He vocalized his meditations in the morning. He made requests (cry) in his meditations. Pay attention to the fact that requests are made in meditation and how this may be key to answered prayers.

Again, he understood what his enemies were doing. And at the end of his meditation, God answered him. God protects and blesses the righteous. Go out from your prayer closet and see the favor that awaits you from people and God. Look back at it during the cool of the day and notice the favor that is like a protective shield surrounding you.

If we seem to see God not answering our prayers, this is not a force-matter issue. Could you be looking in the wrong place or standing where you cannot see?

If we feel forsaken and left alone, should we not check our emotions and straighten them with His counsel? We should never think that God will contradict His promises.

> I was young and now I am old, yet I have never seen the righteous forsaken or their children begging for bread.
>
> ∞ Psalm 37:25 NIV ∞

MEDITATING THROUGH THE BIBLE

Before we find fault with heaven or ourselves, let's change the way we discover our findings, especially if they are contradictory. It is forever established that God changes not. It is evident then, if we see the contrary, that our perception is not correct.

A great example is Job. In his testing, God required the devil to abide by the following:

> And the LORD said unto Satan, Behold, all that he hath is in thy power; only upon himself put not forth thine hand. So, Satan went forth from the presence of the LORD.
>
> ∞ Job 1:12 KJV ∞

From this permission, the devil decimated everything that was associated with Job. His children lost their lives and so did his pets. It was only Job and his wife that remained. Friends who came to console him valiantly looked for confessions of sin and Job's hidden iniquity. The confession they wanted did not come. Instead, Job filled his mouth with words, some without knowledge.

The fact of the matter is that all we have and possess can be within the reach of the evil one. Read again the Job 1:12. Our flesh is not who we are. Satan touched Job's flesh and afflicted him sorely.

At some point, Job confessed he had rashly complained to God and before his friends. At the end Job learned to say what God was saying to him.

DOES GOD CONSIDER YOUR MEDITATION?

> Then JOB said to the Lord, "I know that You can do all things and that no thought or purpose of Yours can be restrained or thwarted. [You said to me] Who is this that darkens and obscures counsel [by words] without knowledge? Therefore [I now see] I have [rashly] uttered what I did not understand, things too wonderful for me, which I did not know. [I had virtually said to You what You have said to me:] Hear, I beseech You, and I will speak; I will demand of You, and You declare to me. I had heard of You [only] by the hearing of the ear, but now my [spiritual] eye sees You.
>
> ∞ Job 42:1-5 AMPC ∞

Job had a key realization when God spoke to him at the end of his sifting. He stood his ground and walked with integrity before all. When it comes to filling your mouth with arguments, complaints or murmurs, make it a few or none before God.

We are better off not speaking what we don't understand, much more so when it is accusations, justifications, and complaints. The children of Israel wandered for 40 years in the wilderness because of these three. These either tell God we have no knowledge and little faith and are not reaching out to seek His wisdom and understand how we can come out of the predicament.

All along to Job who was in a predicament, it looked like this:

> God hath delivered me to the ungodly and turned me over into the hands of the wicked.
>
> ∞ Job 16:11 KJV ∞

MEDITATING THROUGH THE BIBLE

God is an ever-present help in times of need, even when all we hear from all angles is silence. In our situations, whether trying or joyous, let's learn how to:

- Meditate with faith!

- Hear God's voice, separating it from our anxieties or excitement.

- Be still and know that He is God

- Recognize how God reveals Himself to us.

- Praise God with confidence in His promises!

- Extol God above our predicaments or celebrations!

- Create a fellowship space with God as the central focus. Many create a throne room space with God as the focus but feel inadequate to approach Him.

- Approach God not for judgment but for grace. No child approaches a parent for judgment but for grace.

- Choose your identity, relationship to God, stance, and attitude in conversations with God wisely.

Chapter 8

PSALM WITH SILENCE EMBEDDED IN IT

> The Lord has made Himself known; He executes judgment; the wicked are snared in the work of their own hands. HIGGAION [meditation]. SELAH [pause, and calmly think of that]!
>
> ∞ Psalm 9:16 AMPC ∞

The Psalms are books of knowledge, wisdom, understanding, meditation, praise, worship of God, and prayer.

Within these writings, there are intentional moments of silence indicated through musical notations. Imagine there is silence by intention included in the exercise of the practice and acts of worship. How is yours punctuated?

For what purpose could these be here? Is your worship or meditation punctuated with moments of silence before God? If not, this chapter is about to get you started doing so.

Imagine talking to someone without a moment to catch your breath. Now, imagine having a *convo* (conversation) with someone where you are the listener, and they continue like a chatterbox without stopping. Is there a benefit to either party? The one speaking may improve their oratory skills but at the expense of the audience.

A pause, to connect with the audience and to connect the audience to the message is imperative and effective. Prayer, worship, and meditation, when done well, are successful two-way communications between the worshiped and the worshiper. Otherwise, they become monologues with debatable benefits.

MEDITATING THROUGH THE BIBLE

The Higgaion and Selah Texts and Moments

Higgaion is thought to be a staff notation like modern musical notation that denotes a pause or period with no instrument sound. Notice these are at the end of a phrase or sentence where the Psalmist is transitioning or connecting expressions. Bible scholars and historians have no exact knowledge of what higgaion means nor that of the word "selah".

Most people have used selah as a word like "amen" or "hallelujah" which have very different meanings from the connotative suggestion of higgaion or selah in the record and performance of a psalm or musical piece.

The first interesting thing about "this notation" is that we do not know its meaning. And secondly, why is it there in the first place? Thirdly, and critically essential, is the fact that there seems to be a hidden mystery about this notation. It is the mystery of a silent zone in the exercise of praise, worship, and meditation. Fourthly, it is a physical text character (a text body) and thus it cannot be ignored where it exists.

The Psalms are a compilation of prayers, worship, praise, and meditations set to a musical background accompanied by various acts of worship such as dance, shouts, bows, etc.

Music is one of the most powerful methods of praise, worship, and meditation that there is. We do not need to only look at David casting out an afflicting spirit upon King Saul, but we can look at modern music's influence on both good and evil among us.

The Realms That Manifest in Praise, Worship or Meditation

We know you can create an atmosphere of enchantment using music, instruments, vocals, or both. Music is the art of sequencing various sound

PSALM WITH SILENCE EMBEDDED IN IT

frequencies over a time element to create a melodic tune. We also know by the teaching of the Scriptures that there are melodies with praise and worship that are poured out of the hosts that stand before the throne of God. The higgaion symbol stands as a symbol of silence and a frequency turn.

There are realms of joy, fulfillment, and blessing that open to the one who practices praise, worship, and meditation. Those well exercised in these realms are people with a profound state of being. This secret is an open one:

> Yet you are holy, enthroned on the praises of Israel.
>
> ∞ Psalm 22:3 ESV ∞

To a worshiper, praising God cannot be a strange feat. It is in the moments of praise and worship that a believer gets to witness the thundering and the bolts of lightning that proceed from the throne of God. It is possible to see heavenly realms, angelic beings, and visions during times of meditation, worship, and praise.

> Above Him stood seraphim, each having six wings: With two wings they covered their faces, with two they covered their feet, and with two they were flying. And they were calling out to one another: "Holy, holy, holy is the LORD of Hosts; all the earth is full of His glory." At the sound of their voices the doorposts and thresholds shook, and the temple was filled with smoke.
>
> ∞ Isaiah 6:2-4 BSB ∞

MEDITATING THROUGH THE BIBLE

It is true that we are transported beyond the music or worship venue into realms of thought and awareness or frenzy that we cannot explain. These realms are beyond the music or worship itself, standing as proof we enter certain realms of realities that exist yet but are not physically tangible. There is a part of us that touches the invisible celestial realms and sometimes we pull inventions we make upon the earth from them.

> All flesh is not the same flesh: but there is one kind of flesh of men, another flesh of beasts, another of fishes, and another of birds. There are also celestial bodies, and bodies terrestrial: but the glory of the celestial is one, and the glory of the terrestrial is another.
>
> ∞ 1 Corinthians 15:39-40 KJV ∞

You could doubt those who have been transported into these realms when your understanding of the experience is limited to dissecting, touching, and feeling an earthly body.

A spiritual body or a celestial body is something altogether different. Though they are rare sightings of celestial bodies, the intentional and visible transformation from one terrestrial into a celestial can never be denied nor can it be said it does not happen. Science has a word for it: phenomenon.

For example, when a stage four cancer suddenly disappears from a patient, given an understanding they have a few days to live. When they are medically checked, no trace or count of cancer can be found in their body. With nothing done to the patient except faith and a rebuke of the devourer, it can only be a phenomenon, a miracle.

PSALM WITH SILENCE EMBEDDED IN IT

When the Apostle Paul writes, he says there are heavenly bodies. He also talks about having been taken into the third heaven. Out-of-body experiences are not easy to fathom to the unbeliever even if they hear about them. The one who has experienced this is also confounded by it at times. How can you explain reasonably well someone who rises from the dead? Does everyone know how to interpret every dream they have? Each of these entities has different characteristics.

> For this corruptible must put on incorruption, and this mortal must put on immortality.
>
> ∞ 1 Corinthians 15:53 KJV ∞

These realms may end up manifesting physically or we may see their result upon those enchanted by them when they experienced them. I would rather be one to enter the realms of the celestial and worship, praise, and meditate there than be a bystander.

The Higgaion and Selah are bodies of text. They are physical in the sense that they are written, spelled out just like the normal words we use. Why are they denoted as silent markers by many scholars? Could these scholars have been wrong about such assumptions?

The scriptures say the seraphim rests not whether it is day or night. This is Isaiah observing the throne room protocols for the short time he was before the throne of God.

The cherubim cover the mercy seat in the temple's most holy place. The seraphim are before God's throne. These are two different functional spaces. Others may argue the throne room is the same as the temple physically. But there are differences.

MEDITATING THROUGH THE BIBLE

In practice, the most holy place seemed a place of silence with only the noise bells on the High Priest's garments and his soft approach to sacrifice. The throne room is a place that is eventful according to Isaiah's description. The outer sections of the temple are not quiet, however, filled with worship, sacrifice, and all. Understanding these differences can help us know how to approach each atmosphere we enter and be in protocol.

Depending on what heavenly environment you are approaching God in, understand the intonations of silence that are called upon you to exercise.

The throne of God is heaven. It is not terrestrial but celestial. His footstool is the earth. In what house or temple can you boldly approach Him?

> Heaven [is] My throne, and earth the footstool for My feet. What [kind of] house can you build for Me, says the Lord, or what is the place in which I can rest?
>
> ∞ Acts 7:49 ∞

As the living temple of the Holy Spirit, He can lead us (from within) to both places.

> Then as I looked, I saw a door standing open in heaven, and the same voice I had heard before spoke to me like a trumpet blast. The voice said, "Come up here, and I will show you what must happen after this."
>
> ∞ Revelation 4:1 NLT ∞

PSALM WITH SILENCE EMBEDDED IN IT

There is no excuse to not build for God a tabernacle to dwell in by accepting the celestial to take habitation in us. This tabernacle is not in the manner the disciples imagined the tabernacles when on Mount Transfiguration. It is built for the Only One, not three.

> He is the Holy Spirit, who leads into all truth. The world cannot receive him, because it isn't looking for him and doesn't recognize him. But you know him, because he lives with you now and later will be in you.
>
> ∞ John 14:17 NLT ∞

The 7<u>th</u> Seal Opening and the Half Hour Silence

Revelation 8 gives us a glimpse of how heaven uses the art of silence from the throne room to its expanse beyond. Revelation 8 says there was silence in heaven for half an hour when the seventh seal was opened.

> WHEN HE [the Lamb] broke open the seventh seal, there was silence for about half an hour in heaven. And I saw the seven angels who stand before God, and they were given seven trumpets.
>
> Then another angel, who had a golden censer, came and stood at the altar. He was given much incense to offer, along with the prayers of all the saints, on the golden altar before the throne. And the smoke of the incense, together with the prayers of the saints, rose up before God from the hand of the angel.

> Then the angel took the censer, filled it with fire from the altar, and hurled it to the earth; and there were peals of thunder, and rumblings, and flashes of lightning, and an earthquake.
>
> ∞ Revelation 8:1-5 AMPC ∞

Take the vivid image of events shown here and apply them in your daily life and redemption story. As Jesus Christ is making intercession for you before God and your prayers come up, watch closely how they are treated and answered.

Silence in any person's life marks a special moment. Just like silence in heaven marked a very special moment. Here the Lamb had completed the opening of the seven seals.

In a sense, Jesus was showing that He had completed the assignment of redemption as set up by the Father. The text of Revelation 5 shows how important these seals were to human redemption. The silence here signified the end of all limitations, all secrets, and all covenants that limited humanity.

Pause for a Moment of Silence

- Imagine all the accusations against you canceled and deemed insufficient against the sacrifice of Jesus and cleared.

- Imagine all critical and incriminating witness testimony having lost the power to stain you. The blood of Jesus has been qualified and is worthy to redeem you.

- Imagine the angelic host ready to make proclamations with the blowing of the trumpet.

- Imagine your prayers and those of all the saints ascend before God.

PSALM WITH SILENCE EMBEDDED IN IT

The mighty angel is given more than enough incense to offer with the prayers on the golden altar. As the incense smoke rises from the golden altar, so do your prayers. Remember nothing is capable of standing before God. Our meditation and prayers are the exception. They arise before Him. They are elevated. This is the reason Jesus says, "Man ought always to pray and not faint".

If Revelation 8 is how God deals with our prayers and this happens before the throne of God, day and night (eternally but shown without limitation of man's day and night), are you leaving too much out of the golden censor by not praying enough? Are your meditation and prayers qualified, based on abiding in the vine and faith in Him, to even be included as the "prayers of …the saints"?

Take time to observe silence before the LORD. More so, let your flesh (earth) be silent.

How does one get to know of a small still voice unless you have penetrated the realm of silence to the extent that the low frequencies of audio are audible and discernable to you? And is this possible in a music setting of any kind? Yes. Is this possible in meditation? Come up hither and see.

> Hush, all flesh, because of Jehovah, For He hath been roused up from His holy habitation!
>
> ∞ Zechariah 2:13 YLT ∞

This all begins with a journey to know the beautiful voices hidden in the silence when one practices to "be still and know that I AM God."

Chapter 9

IS YOUR MEDITATION ONE FROM THE HEART?

> Let the words of my mouth and the meditation of my heart be acceptable in Your sight, O Lord, my [firm, impenetrable] Rock, and my Redeemer.
>
> ∞ Psalm 19:14 AMPC ∞

Our words, from our mouths, are like pictures or a live video feed that plays out in ultra-high definition before God. It is almost impossible to picture words oozing out from a mouth without a series of thoughts that are acting as the intelligence behind them.

Thoughts are, scientifically, the result of complex interactions between neurons in the brain which when interacting produce electromagnetic fields from the small electric currents resulting from their interactions. How thoughts influence the process of imagination, inspiration, sensory input and reaction, innovation, and past experiences we can wonder. Thoughts inform and control bodily actions, speaking, and the acting out of the thoughts.

It is without question that if the words of my mouth are to be acceptable in God's sight, then so are my thoughts. The advantage we all have is that thoughts are the fastest element of unseen activities of humans. Thoughts have the ability to debate themselves in one's brain and heart before they ooze out. They can regulate and self-contain the little rascals, or the little rascals can overpower the goodwill angels by tying them up in knots (or is it naughts?) of confusion.

We all know what happens when the misfits find liberty to be mouthed. They unleash fiascoes and tribulations leaving the goodwill angels to come later to apologize and make amends.

MEDITATING THROUGH THE BIBLE

Notice that the reference to "the words of my mouth" is not limited to during meditation in this text. Instead, what we speak with our mouths at any time and our eventual meditation should both be acceptable to God.

What is worth noting from Psalm 19 is that we can meditate from the heart. Since meditation is an act of pondering deeply, it is a focusing act. It is without controversy one can do it from the mind as a series of thoughts. But if this has no root depth to the heart, you can utter the words, but they are like sound waves with no decipherable message.

It is certainly difficult to think of something being done from the heart and the same be lacking in intent unless it is idle thought. Have intention when words come out of your mouth, whether in meditation or in conversation.

More than having intentions, weigh the good of your intention. Judge your thoughts and imagination. Check your own heart. If you speak your thoughts without assessment, do not blame other people for assessing it for you.

When others are speaking, try not to be the bad judge. Firstly, decipher their intention. Be slow to answer. You do not need to necessarily agree with everyone and everything and neither is there an eternal imperative for you to disagree.

If your intention is not good, be careful to repent promptly rather than let God correct your waywardness.

In the general court of law, what you say before another individual binds you. In like manner, the words of your mouth are binding before God. Be careful of your thoughts.

IS YOUR MEDITATION ONE FROM THE HEART?

> THE PLANS of the mind and orderly thinking belong to man, but from the Lord comes the [wise] answer of the tongue. All the ways of a man are pure in his own eyes, but the Lord weighs the spirits (the thoughts and intents of the heart)
>
> ∞ Proverbs 16:1-2 AMP ∞

Before God, thoughts speak equally as loud as words mouthed. Though not spoken as long as it is in your heart, God sees it. What? Does God then communicate with our thoughts?

Allow your heart to be prepared by God to carry answers to questions only God can answer. If one cannot submit their heart to His Holy Spirit sent from the presence of God, how can they be submitted to God who sits upon His throne? The best way to make God's throne and His presence accessible is to become the temple of His Holy Spirit.

Storing up God's Word in one's heart cannot happen without God speaking to one's heart or that Word being written therein. And God's Word stored in the original intent and form of the word is Spirit, giving its Life to the heart that accepts it. (John 6:63)

> I have stored up your word in my heart, that I might not sin against you.
>
> ∞ Psalm 119:11 ESV ∞

MEDITATING THROUGH THE BIBLE

This we find then that meditating from the heart requires first a good deposit. When a good deposit exists in the heart, the thoughts and intents come out circumspect. Thinking good thoughts and being mindful of the presence of God inside of the earthen vessel brings into subjection to good things our emotions and thirsts.

To be far removed from self-condemnation or others' exercise in seeing us this way, one must have confidence in God. Remember Job.

> Beloved, if our heart does not condemn us, we have confidence before God; and whatever we ask we receive from him, because we keep his commandments and do what pleases him.
>
> ∞ 1 John 3:21-22 ESV ∞

Jesus died on the cross to do away with our past. We confess all our sins and our failures to Him. We leave it all there and He takes it away from us and from His memory eternally. It is like our sins and failures have never existed. Why fish for them again? *(a good reference to read on thoughts and beliefs is from Chapter 12 of the book Supernal Grace, by Elenah Kangara)*

To receive what we ask of God, we must immerse ourselves in our identity in Him and have faith that all our needs have already been provided. It is through awakening to this truth and practicing the art of silence in meditation that we prevent any sense of lack. This quiet contemplation helps us connect deeply with our spiritual essence, allowing us to fully realize the abundance already present within us.

Jesus, teaching said, "No man can serve two masters". Who does your heart serve? Who do the words of your mouth serve? Are you inclined to both

IS YOUR MEDITATION ONE FROM THE HEART?

faith and doubt, feeding either one or both to suit convenience and advantage? There is a word for this; lukewarm, fence-sitting, or mediocre. This is a Laodicean condition (Revelation 3:14-21).

The Laodicean condition leads to spiritual blindness, poverty, and nakedness. It can be so comfortable that one feels they do not need anything until a moment of reckoning arrives. How can you receive healing or deliverance when there is no coherent intent to do so?

In all you do, let your yes be so, and your no be a firm no. The door to blessings is completely shut against a double-minded person. Seek the Tree of Life without wanting to experience the fruit from the tree of the knowledge of good and evil.

> But when you ask, you must believe and not doubt, because the one who doubts is like a wave of the sea, blown and tossed by the wind. That person should not expect to receive anything from the Lord. Such a person is double-minded and unstable in all they do.
>
> ∞ James 1:6-8 NIV ∞

God is pleased by our faith when we come before Him. He is more than pleased with profound faith if we constantly dwell in His secret place before Him. We know heaven to be a spiritual and physical place from its descriptions, dreams, and visions. In heaven's vastness and dimensions (levels), there is a secret place of the Most High. The earth too is both physical and spiritual. It has its secret places as well.

Faith should be top on your checklist about your meditation being accepted before God.

Chapter 10

WHERE DO YOU DWELL AT ALL TIMES?

> One thing have I asked of the Lord, that will I seek, inquire for, and [insistently] require: that I may dwell in the house of the Lord [in His presence] all the days of my life, to behold and gaze upon the beauty [the sweet attractiveness and the delightful loveliness] of the Lord and to meditate, consider, and inquire in His temple.
>
> ∞ Psalm 27:4 AMPC ∞

Have you ever asked yourself any of the following 5 questions?

1. What have you earnestly asked of the LORD?
2. What have you earnestly sought after in life?
3. What do you expect daily from the LORD and life?
4. What have you given to the world from your heart?
5. Taking into conscious account that you are spirit, where do you dwell as a spirit?

These questions look very simple to answer except for the last one. And indeed, they are. We all know what we want, need and what we can give, at superficial or deep levels. Our thoughts and our hearts dwell in these desires.

But here David showed us a different place where we should dwell. Psalm 27 is one of those deep insightful scriptures that makes us self-introspect.

Where our flesh dwells matter. This is why we build beautiful houses.

What we are attracted to and delighted with matters. This is why we dress and adorn ourselves elegantly.

MEDITATING THROUGH THE BIBLE

What we yearn to eat and be satisfied with matters. The culinary world is expansive and intriguing, yet our stomach and palate are not multiplied.

Our mental faculties are in continuous research and discovery. What we feed our mind with matters.

The lust of the flesh is the greed that every human must tame and turn its use for good. The lust of the eyes, being superficial and not spiritual, always leads to the tree of the knowledge of the good and the evil. The pride of life is suffocating to the spirit.

Life is spiritual and the flesh taking pride when the spiritual is not crowned in any life causes people to misplace priorities. The flesh should not be a god over the spirit. No parent is without greed when it concerns their children. No patriot is without preferential bias towards their country.

These three evils (lusts) are a weariness to the spirit of a human. They are the direct cause of sin and separation from God. Psalm 27 teaches spiritual self-care.

We should prioritize our spiritual matters. The presence of the LORD is a dwelling place we should be always in. The presence of the LORD should not be confused with the congregation, synagogue, or sensation of awe, a vision, or a dream. All these are places and instances where you may meet God, but they are not the dwelling place of His Person.

> However, the Most High does not dwell in houses and temples made with hands; as the prophet says, "Heaven [is] My throne, and earth the footstool for My feet. What [kind of] house can you build for Me, says the Lord, or what is the place in which I can rest?
>
> Was it not My hand that made all these things?"
>
> ∞ Acts 7:48-50 AMPC ∞

WHERE DO YOU DWELL AT ALL TIMES?

It follows, that if God does not dwell in temples made by human hands, and He is Spirit (John 4:24), then His dwelling is, in a similar fashion, the dwelling place of the human spirit at a minimum.

At the highest level of understanding God's dwelling place is sophisticated beyond human flesh, soul, and spirit understanding. If the heavens are just God's throne, who can tell of His dwelling?

What we stumble at is not that the heavens are God's throne and the earth His footstool. We fall and fail because of the simplicity of the place God has revealed as His dwelling place. Conjuring up His greatness, we fumble when He comes to us in simplicity. The world looked for the Messiah back then and stumbled at His coming as a baby born in a manger. God comes in simplicity and often our innkeeper has no room for Him in our spirit, hearts, and minds.

How can the Creator of all dwell in a baby? In Jesus? Did the God of all really put His Name upon Yeshua? How can there be Father, Son, and the Holy Spirit and be one God and LORD? How can the Father, Jesus, and the Holy Spirit come and live within me? Where are They coming from? Are They leaving Heaven or whatever Their place empty? If They abide with me, how can They then abide with billions of other people who believe in them?

> Jesus answered, If a person [really] loves Me, he will keep My word [obey My teaching]; and My Father will love him, and We will come to him and make Our home (abode, special dwelling place) with him.
>
> ∞ John 14:23 AMPC ∞

MEDITATING THROUGH THE BIBLE

You do not need to tie your human mind with projections. These projections try to put God at the mercy of the gravitational forces of the earth. They also attempt to bind God to the forces of the universe. God is Spirit, as Jesus taught in John 4:24.

You cannot containerize God into a body of flesh. Nor can you confine God to the expanse of your spirit. He is greater and more sophisticated than you can imagine Him to be.

There are many other limitations that do not apply to God. God has not required sacrifice from us but a yielded spirit, soul, and body that He can dwell in. If you can receive Him, then do so and learn to be different from your former thoughts, wisdom, and understanding. If you think limiting thoughts of who HE is, then that is the extent to which He can only reveal Himself to you.

Should He give you more understanding than you are willing to retain when He knows that what you do not retain, you throw away? Why expect God to give His whole person, counsel, and wisdom when it is too lofty for you?

Start your journey of God abiding with you by believing He can. He is indwelling. Begin to experience the awesomeness of who He is through meditation.

Where you, as a person, more than your thoughts of what is flesh, soul, and spirit, dwell matters. Find habitation in God and likewise, give habitation to God and you will see the goodness of God.

You will show me the path of life; in Your presence is fullness of joy, at Your right hand there are pleasures forevermore.

∞ Psalm 16:11 AMPC ∞

WHERE DO YOU DWELL AT ALL TIMES?

Naturally, the lack of self-care is often a sign of deeper concerns. The same holds true for spiritual neglect. When both physical and spiritual self-care are absent, a person becomes like a ship without sails—directionless and vulnerable. This absence can manifest in low self-esteem, burnout, physical health issues, anxiety, stress, fear, unstable faith, and even misplaced admiration of others.

Bear in mind that worry about self-care is captivating and crippling. This is why Jesus says "Take no thought" about what you shall eat, drink, wear, and where you shall sleep. Use what you have and act on what you are capable of in "the now" moment. God never used what Moses did not have to make him successful before Pharaoh. A shepherd's rod and the palm of Moses' hand were enough when he proclaimed God's word.

If you so dwell in him and He dwells in you, you lack nothing. God lacks not. The key to manifesting what you pray for lies in where you dwell more than faithing it.

> He that dwelleth in the secret place of the Most High shall abide under the shadow of the Almighty.
>
> ∞ Psalm 91: 1 KJV ∞

> Because you have made the Lord your refuge, and the Most High your dwelling place, there shall no evil befall you, nor any plague or calamity come near your tent.
>
> ∞ Psalm 91:9-10 KJV ∞

This is what Job sought (Job 23:4-6) and when he had removed his spirit from the ash heap into the presence of God, the chains of calamity were broken. Call those things that are not yet manifest as if they are.

The ASK Principle Meditation

The LORD is in you, His holy temple. If so, the fleshly desires (your earth) will not have preeminence upon your life.

> But the Lord is in His holy temple; let all the earth hush and keep silence before Him.
>
> ∞ Habakkuk 2:20 AMPC ∞

As Paul says, "Christ in you is the hope of your glory". Notice, that Paul says Christ, meaning the Word of God made manifest in the present time. God is not manifesting Himself to those who do not believe in Him dwelling in them.

> If you abide in me, and my words abide in you, ask for whatever you wish, and it will be done for you.
>
> ∞ John 15:7 NRSV ∞

WHERE DO YOU DWELL AT ALL TIMES?

The devil believes in God and trembles at His name, though he tries to fool human beings as being fearless of God. But God does not dwell in the devil because of the devil's unbelief. This unbelief manifests ill intentions towards God and mankind. God will not permit His Spirit to dwell in Satan because of his rebellion. The devil's actions reveal the absence of God within him.

If you claim to believe God and God truly dwells in you, then your works should reflect His presence. Where is the love for His creation? Where is the pursuit of peace with all people? If the fruit of your life in these things is sweet, then blessed are you. If not, God does not cast away the one who turns from evil works to do good.

Examine your heart and your intentions. Do not be like the evil one who hates God and His creation. Let your life testify to the One who lives within you. This is why we are admonished to seek first God's kingdom and righteousness.

Jesus taught about the ASK principle in this manner:

> Ask, and it shall be given you; seek, and ye shall find; knock, and it shall be opened unto you: For everyone that asketh receiveth; and he that seeketh findeth; and to him that knocketh it shall be opened
>
> ∞ Matthew 7:7-8 KJV ∞

A	**ASK** and it shall be given
S	**SEEK** and ye shall find
K	**KNOCK** and it shall be opened

MEDITATING THROUGH THE BIBLE

In the emphasis Jesus wanted to show on this, He talks about a son and a father. The son asked his father for bread. Notice that children of a father dwell in the house with their father. This is a basic humanity principle He did not mention. We do not throw our children out of the house. We do not give our children a stone for bread. Our modern-day societies have made children casualties of a father's provision as most fathers play truants from their children.

No wonder Jesus rebuked Satan when Satan asked that Jesus turn stones into bread. Jesus's hunger before God could not be satisfied with Jesus' laboring to turn stones into bread. Neither does our hunger before God become fulfilled similarly. The herb, seed, fruit, and harvest times were prepositioned to meet our needs before we came to the garden.

Jesus dwelt in the Father and the Father dwelt in Him. Jesus' meditation day and night was in the Father.

> While he was still speaking, behold, a bright cloud overshadowed them; and suddenly a voice came out of the cloud, saying, "This is My beloved Son, in whom I am well pleased. Hear Him!"
>
> ∞ Matthew 17:5 NKJV ∞

Having shown here where Jesus dwelt and where everyone who believes should dwell, let me bring you back to Psalm 27. Read this whole chapter being mindful of where you dwell. Follow through with the text written in this chapter.

And at every turn, believe that you are in Christ Jesus. As Jesus is in the Father, so are you. Being filled with His Spirit, He dwells in you.

WHERE DO YOU DWELL AT ALL TIMES?

God has not outsourced His fatherhood towards us to some forgetful principal. Unfortunately, it's those who are his children that are negligent of their estate as His children. If we are conscious of being in Him and that God is in us, we will realize that *most things we need in life have already been provided.*

> You keep him in perfect peace whose mind is stayed on you, because he trusts in you.
>
> ∞ Isaiah 26:3 ESV ∞

Find peace. Dwell in the secret place. Meditate on where you dwell. Take corrective measures to not disqualify yourself by choosing to be *an in-transit dweller*. This is what Satan specializes in, *"going up and down and to-and-from upon the earth"*.

No one can believe God for you. Either you believe or you don't. Either you know or you don't. We perish for lack of knowledge.

> Peace: I leave with you; My [own] peace I now give and bequeath to you. Not as the world gives do I give to you. Do not let your hearts be troubled, neither let them be afraid. [Stop allowing yourselves to be agitated and disturbed; and do not permit yourselves to be fearful and intimidated and cowardly and unsettled.]
>
> ∞ John 14:27 AMPC ∞

Shalom! Peace! Dwell! From the LORD Himself, receive it.

Chapter 11

AGAINST THE MEDITATORS OF TREACHERY

> They also that seek and demand my life lay snares for me, and they that seek and require my hurt speak crafty and mischievous things; they meditate treachery and deceit all the day long.
>
> ∞ Psalm 38:12 AMPC ∞

Are you engaging in a treacherous habit of not meditating? Why is this question addressed towards you and not "they"?

In a kingdom, to act against that kingdom's principles of government and leadership is an act of treason.

Consider yourself a kingdom. If you do things that put you into a demise or a loss paradigm, you are betraying your kingdom.

Look at King David. He had imperial guards and a military protecting him. This did not assuage any of his enemies from laying snares against him.

I am not sure at what point in David's life he wrote Psalm 38 and if all this was a direct story of the affliction he was suffering. If this was known, we could accurately see what was happening to David to write and sing such a Psalm. I am inclined to suggest that this fits the time when King Saul was hunting David day in and day out (1 Samuel 19) or the time of Absalom's rebellion (2 Samuel 15 through 19).

David had been in King Saul's household before he became king. He fled from Saul's house because Saul had physically exercised an intent to kill him several times. Saul set up traps, sent spies, and tried to use enticing words to lay ahold of David's life to no avail.

David had been around Ahithophel and the army of Israel more than Absalom had been. Absalom forsook God, "the Father of peace" (the meaning of his name, Avshalom), and slew his brother Amnon earlier in life. Now, he wanted the throne and King David's head on a platter. Talk of a child having a murderous intent on a parent.

David knew that these characters were men that meditated. Unfortunately, they extended their meditation into treachery and deceit against those who stood in their way.

There are people who do this day in day out without any shame. They are the King Ahab and Jezebel, the hardened Pharaoh and the rich man who despised Lazarus the beggar and ended up eternally in the flames of fire. The list does not end with Biblical characters. It also includes kings and leaders who professed Christianity.

To them, the end where they are victorious justifies the cruel and evil means they use(d) to get to the top. One easily identifiable trait about such people is they do not serve the plight of the needy nor do they regard the God of the widow, the poor and the orphan. To them, the needy have no God but them. You cannot find any crumbs at their table for the poor. Their dogs will have eaten them because they too are famished.

Absalom did terrible things in the sight of the kingdom against his father's household and his father's concubines. Ahithophel's advice was obnoxious (2 Samuel 16:20-23). Here a man whose advice was once like the counsel of God but now was deep in the weeds, smoking something from the spirits of indecency. Hushai, a loyal counsel of King David, concerned himself with scattering the well-thought-out plans of Ahithophel to defeat King David. Thank God for Hushai.

AGAINST THE MEDITATORS OF TREACHERY

> For when the world with all its earthly wisdom failed to perceive and recognize and know God by means of its own philosophy, God in His wisdom was pleased through the foolishness of preaching [salvation, procured by Christ and to be had through Him], to save those who believed (who clung to and trusted in and relied on Him).
>
> For while Jews [demandingly] ask for signs and miracles and Greeks pursue philosophy and wisdom,
>
> We preach Christ (the Messiah) crucified, [preaching which] to the Jews is a scandal and an offensive stumbling block [that springs a snare or trap], and to the Gentiles it is absurd and utterly unphilosophical nonsense.
>
> But to those who are called, whether Jew or Greek (Gentile), Christ [is] the Power of God and the Wisdom of God.
>
> ∞ 1 Corinthians 1:21-24 AMPC ∞

Not every friend or trusted counsel is necessary when you are faced with the question, "What should I do? Give me your advice". The one who dwells in the LORD is best served enquiring from the LORD. Compare the advice of trusted confidants with the standard raised from the good intent of your heart by God.

MEDITATING THROUGH THE BIBLE

Imagination and Meditation That God Put a Stop to

The Spirit of God is not one given to strive with mankind. Most of the time we make prayers of "warfare" where it seems the target is to change God's mind rather than fight against powers and principalities of the dark.

> Then the LORD saw that the wickedness of man was great upon the earth, and that every inclination of the thoughts of his heart was altogether evil all the time. And the LORD regretted that He had made man on the earth, and He was grieved in His heart.
>
> ∞ Genesis 6:5-6 BSB ∞

It was not enough for God to cut the years of the life of humans to a 120-year span. Our generations are in a much shorter lifespan than Noah's. God had to stop the people of Noah's time because of their imagination (clearly a form of meditation).

If our intent is not right, our thoughts are louder than our "filtered" or "educated uttered words" in the ears of God. If then our words are as evil, unrestrained, and bellicose as our thoughts, can we blame God when He judges our uncouth behaviors?

What are the inclinations of the thoughts of your heart like? Remember Jesus in Matthew 5 amplifies what the law could not amplify. Are you calling your sister or brother "Raca"? What about unforgiveness? Are you busy asking God for something and yet you hold vendettas unforgivingly towards the closest person to you?

We live in a super age where the whole counsel of God is at our fingertips. We don't necessarily need to hear God's voice to know what He values.

AGAINST THE MEDITATORS OF TREACHERY

Look in the mirror of His Word and see yourself through His lens. If you are willing to not fool yourself, you know very well what inclinations you should shake off.

Desist from living life being influenced by thoughts that justify decadence and lust. When looking at what you exhibit, is this how a loving God made you? How can we excuse anger, malfeasance, maleficence, murder, orphaning the little ones, enslaving the poor, etc?

The progression of human civilization speaks against some of the premeditated acts of corruption and departure from what is civil. Having thoughts that are evil all the time is not criminal in a court of law, if not acted upon, but before God this is a red flag. It is easy to change the law to accommodate human weakness, if all legislators and judicial officers deem it fit.

Continuously evil thoughts will normalize abominable acts among mankind in the sight of God. When this is done in agreement, God can only intervene to stop it. This was the fate of Noah's time, the tower of Babel, and the fall of Sodom and Gomorrah.

At no time has God asked us to excuse our weaknesses. He asks us to eschew evil and sin. We should be careful about what we are establishing with our thoughts.

Chapter 12

WISDOM, UNDERSTANDING, & THE HEART

> My mouth shall speak wisdom, and the meditation of my heart shall be understanding.
>
> ∞ Psalm 49:3 AMPC ∞

What are your examples of understanding? How is your understanding arrived at? What informs your understanding?

I won't delve deeply into wisdom here. I will touch on it briefly in the last chapter of this book. God willing, I will cover in depth what I understand as wisdom, from a biblical perspective, in a future volume.

One of the most successful kings in recorded history is the shepherd boy who rose to lead Israel as its king. King David's humble beginnings are not a myth. The scriptures record that God took him from following herds of bleating sheep on the grasslands to the pinnacle position in the palace of Israel.

Imagine, most of your youth you have been hiding either from the incessant rain or blistering sun in a cave or makeshift shelter close to the grazing pastures. Then just by the pouring out of oil by a prophet, and a few words (if any) your whole focus and strength leaps and bounces into slaying giants, winning wars, and celebrity warrior status in a short period. How do you acquire wisdom and understanding to stay on assignment and not lose yourself?

MEDITATING THROUGH THE BIBLE

The Importance of Meditation of the Heart

Meditation of the heart is imperative to staying the course. If you do not search your heart, how can you know your heart and keep it from greed? It is good to ask God to search your heart. It is even better to ask God to do this after you have already searched it yourself and have turned away from any wickedness in advance.

Having initiative is golden when you want to build character, succeed and prosper in life while grounded in favor with God.

Here we find a secret of being a child of God who is molded in similitude to and models God's own heart. God prepares a continuing dominion for all who seek after his own heart and who keep His voice. Saul's lineage got cut off, but David's continues and is expanded to this day.

We should examine our love for God and His people if our time of peace and fellowship with God begins to be impacted by a discontinued favor from God and our atmosphere.

> But now your kingdom shall not continue. The LORD has sought for Himself a man after His own heart, and the LORD has commanded him to be commander over His people because you have not kept what the LORD commanded you.
>
> ∞ 1 Samuel 13:14 NKJV ∞

King Saul had a lackluster attitude towards God's word and direction for him. He was putting the realm of God's people in peril and his dominion was cut short.

WISDOM, UNDERSTANDING, & THE HEART

If we come upon seasons of testing, we lack, our worship and giving alms should continue with better quality and judgment. To spiritually search one's own heart, know it, and root out any evil should not be postponed to a session when it is revealed by someone, a prophet or servant of God.

It is not that God desires to withhold anything good from us. Will it benefit us if we gain the whole world and yet be without a soul?

We have seen repressive political systems where abject hunger, corruption, and murder are the three evils that await a nation day after day. It gets worse than hell when the masses adopt a me-first attitude and there is lawlessness. The widow and the orphan end up dispossessed even the little they had.

But when people can pray, worship, and meditate with all their heart and act upon their convictions to do good, they have better solutions to allay calamity. They have the better perception to keep out of their leadership any perverse leader. The expectations of the wicked will never come to fruition (Proverbs 10:28)

A life of heartfelt prayer, worship, and meditation is like an anti-evil-rain umbrella. This kind of life checks all the boxes that God's precepts require and an invisible hedge of protection against evil will border such a person. It is impossible to be denied by God when you meditate from the heart and are aligned with His will. Excellence dwells where alignment with God exists.

MEDITATING THROUGH THE BIBLE

Key Meditation of the Heart Points

- Be vigilant against your mind bringing thoughts straying from a full self-examination.

- Do not look at superficial reasons/feelings and end there when self-examining!

- Find root causes/reasons good or bad that hinder you from becoming the best you. Sometimes these may be dormant principalities that feed superficial ones. Unshackle from the bad and extol the good.

- Find what traits feed the weaknesses you discover about yourself more than they feed the strengths you have.

- Feed your strengths more. Start a rebellion against your weaknesses by abandoning or redirecting tendencies once captured by a weakness to feed your strengths.

- Stand against the mindset that says you are not able, concerning the good things which you have thought you are incapable of

- Confess that you can, you will, and you do believe and can do better and greater than you see now.

- When now expressing worship and adoration to God, be aware of your nearness to Him.

- What is your understanding of the heart of God towards His people? How does your heart and intention measure towards all people in the face of the love of God for them?

- In the face of the test question that fails your life's enterprise and love for God if you hate your fellow human you see, what changes do you need to enforce in your life to come on the right track?

Chapter 13

NIGHT WATCHES AND MEDITATING ON GOD

> When I remember thee upon my bed, and meditate on thee in the night-watches.
>
> ∞ Psalm 63:6 ASV ∞

We could all be excused when we think the bed is for sleeping and not meditation. Some believe that the bed is not made to remember the LORD upon it because of how they have lived and seen others live.

But conversely, see what kind of a workshop your mind becomes if you choose not to retain the acknowledgment of the LORD in your mind. The bed must be undefiled by thoughts and by acts carried out while it is in use.

Modern time bedtime moments have either a book, a smartphone, or a television show to contend with for the first watch.

The Hebrew traditions have for ages kept a system of night watches. Imagine the beauty of waking up to meditate! What beauty? At first, I saw myself too deeply intoxicated with sleep in the heat of the lull to even open my eyes and be aware I could meditate or pray. Is it good to meditate? Then it is good to believe I can do this. I will do it if I believe I can.

> My eyes anticipate the night watches, and I am awake before the cry of the watchman, that I may meditate on Your word.
>
> ∞ Psalm 119:148 AMPC ∞

MEDITATING THROUGH THE BIBLE

These watches of the night are a system of dividing the night into different periods. This system was used by the ancient Hebrews and is mentioned here in Psalm 63:6 and 119:148.

Some watchmen keep watch of the nighttime security of their villages in many communities around the world.

In the African village, men keep their ears open mainly for the sound of hyenas and jackals that come to steal, kill, and destroy their domestic animals in the kraal.

To this day, some Jewish groups, Christians and others still engage in worship, prayer, meditation or spiritual acts tying these to the night watches. The children of Israel used a three-watch system where the night was divided into three watches:

- The first watch: sunset to ten (10 PM) o'clock,
- the second watch: ten (10 PM) o'clock to two (2 AM) in the morning,
- and the third watch: two (2 AM) o'clock to sunrise

How in the world were these observed before clocks were invented? Hebrew generations used basic elements in their environment as a call to remember the LORD and meditate:

- 1st watch- the bray of a donkey/the neigh of a horse
- 2nd watch- howl of a dog
- 3rd watch- the time for a baby to nurse from its mother.

NIGHT WATCHES AND MEDITATING ON GOD

Other societies have used the crowing of the cock to identify these times. Jesus told Peter about how he would deny Him before the cock crowed the third time. At the third crow, Peter realized he had warmed himself too much at the fire of Jesus' accusers.

Outside of these elements, the human body is also equipped with the capacity for moments of conscious turning in the night. These may also coincide with bathroom visit moments for some.

Meditation elevates your communion with God to higher realms. It is the best way to have a vibrant relationship with God. For here one can fellowship with God beyond what worship and prayer can enable when engaged without meditation.

A man and woman, dating or otherwise, who spend more time communicating with each other and doing things together develop a deep relationship. The depth of your personal relationship with God is not based on how much time you spend serving Him. The time spent serving God is a profound ministration period, as you become a conduit of His grace to others.

I am not saying that the one who serves then does not know God. There are levels of knowledge informed by the kind of relationship and experiences between two individuals. The communion that happens beyond formal roles between two people deepens friendships, romance, feelings, knowledge, wisdom, and understanding of each other.

The time you take to personally experience and know God, as a being, not serving Him, is arrived at through the meditation of the heart. This was Adam's way of communing with God in the cool of the day and reflecting on Him as he lay down to rest.

One who is only serving God without closeness of experience and friendship sees a master-servant relationship while the one who is intimately related sees a deeper relationship informed by a family tie or friendship tie. It is easier to refine one's actions, outlook, and character through a deep mutual understanding and knowledge informed by fellowship experience.

What are some of the traditions, customs, and behavioral traits that inform your understanding of the night watches? Do you value the moments you consciously turn while asleep or when you awaken from dream and realize what has been?

When each of my children were still suckling babies, their cribs were right by my side. They sometimes slept on my chest after feeding or if they had been restless.

Can you picture yourself coming before God, not in the throne room as a servant but as a child putting your head in His lap and falling asleep? Why not? Is this not the place a child should aspire to be to lay aside all fears, anxieties, or concerns?

> It is vain for you to rise up early, to take rest late, to eat the bread of [anxious] toil—for He gives [blessings] to His beloved in sleep.
>
> ∞ Psalm 127:2 APMC ∞

The big question is, how do you remember God when you are in your bed? Do you meditate at all in the night watches? Make it a habit to be conscious of God and worship him.

See the vast landscape of God's intentions for you as you remember Him. He comes in and sups with you. He reveals Himself to you.

NIGHT WATCHES AND MEDITATING ON GOD

Open your dreamscape wide to God and His heavenly realm. Remembering the LORD and meditating on Him in the night watch opens you up to opportunities to receive blessings from Him in your sleep. It is your meditation and your remembrance of Him in the night watches that transports you into His realities. God will not take you where you are not willing to go by faith.

Chapter 14

MEDITATION AND THAT SONG IN THE NIGHT

> I call to remembrance my song in the night; with my heart I meditate and my spirit searches diligently:
>
> ∞ Psalm 77:6 ∞

Your song in the night, what is it like? Is it praise? Is it worship? Is it an infatuation with your idols of love, lust or greed? What truly fills your heart in those quiet hours?

Is your nighttime filled with glee? Is it filled with forgetfulness because you are either having so much fun or in so much anguish?

Is your nighttime filled with cries and groaning? Is there bitterness in your life because of the place where you are?

There is a time for everything. It is the cry of the watchman that we must tune our ears to in the nighttime and not so much our own.

The night watches are for singing melodies in your heart. Your spirit is created with a program to search diligently on issues about you, God, your assignment, and your community. You position your heart to receive answers to the things your spirit searches for by meditating in this portion of time. Though weeping may endure for the night, there is no record that weeping should eclipse the moments of the song in the night.

A person that goes to sleep having made peace with God and their family, is surely bound to hear from God clearly than a heart heavy with sorrow. If you wake up in the morning and see no change in your circumstances, then that's your time to cry out. After all, His mercies are new every morning.

The king of Aram sent an army in the nighttime to capture Elisha. But a powerful army cannot contend with the power of one who meditated and worshiped in the night watches to gain the glory of an earthly king against the God of heaven.

They surrounded the city of Dothan, where Elisha was staying with his servant. However, Elisha was surrounded by an invisible heavenly army bigger and more lethal than the visible arm of the Arameans. The army sent to capture him ended up captured by Elisha and was handed to the king of Israel.

Be intentional with your night watches. Choose wisely who visits you physically and spiritually. What you watch, read, and listen to. The shackles of nightmares, demonic visitations, and witchcraft cannot stand and win against a child of God who is in tune to the frequency of God's voice.

One of the things most common in religion is a believer afflicting their soul or flesh. There are vexations which believers have accepted as a spiritual exercise fulfilling to God and them. Stern-faced, not able to smile, and not affable, they afflict their souls and their bodies, not for obedience to God but to appear dedicated.

If you look in the mirror and recognize how you have isolated, afflicted, and imprisoned yourself against your own better judgment, how can you expect God to honor such self-inflicted suffering as a dedication to Him?

Use this question as a meditation to self-determine how you have created a life song and reset your life to engage in the gladness of the heart.

Should we forget about "rejoice in the LORD always" and "Again, I say rejoice"? Rejoicing in the LORD means what it means. Move out of self. Move your whole being and be in the LORD. And here, you cannot help it but to rejoice. Those who enter in and abide can never say "No" to God.

I have traversed in a song in the night countless times. Also, most of the songs, poems, and writings I have done came to me in the nighttime. It has been my way of worship from as early as 1987, just two years after I

MEDITATION AND THAT SONG IN THE NIGHT

accepted the LORD Jesus Christ as my Savior. I was not aware I was engaging in meditation then and for some years that followed.

As I was meditating and scribbling my notes on this subject in the night, here is one song I sang to God Almighty:

>Yes, yes, yes, yes.
>Amen, Amen, Amen,
>Glory, Glory, Glory
>El, Eli, Elohim

>CHORUS:
>My God, I praise You
>You are my King
>You are my LORD
>And You are my Strength

>My Song in the Night
>I belong to You
>I remember You,
>El, Eli, Elohim

Sometimes, I have woken up to go to a keyboard and play what I have been singing or playing in a dream. Sometimes, it is songs that we already know that come to remembrance. The fellowship with God in these moments is profound.

Start by offering worship to God with your song in the night. Sometimes, these are songs sung in silence in the deep of the night. If you are engaged in meditation in this way, you will not fail to see God's guidance and visitation when He so wishes or you so desire it. Your spirit engages the search mode every time you meditate from the heart. And those that seek Him find Him.

If we were to talk about dreams, visions, and encounters with God or His host, time and space would fail us. God has ministered not only to me through dreams but to others through dreams He has given.

There are instances when encounters are so palpable, that it literary feels like you just stepped out from another world or atmosphere into the normal one.

The more we surrender worshipfully and meditatively, the more capacity God gives to inspire our lives.

Do not only do this for the sake of trying to get a message to minister to God's people. Choose it as a lifestyle of experiencing God for yourself. It will ground you and you will not question your faith in Him. Neither can any trials shake you. Choose God for you first before seeking to want to tell others what God is saying when you are not even encountering Him.

If you have such a close communion with God, you will not misconstrue God's intent, His way of working with His people, and His mercy and grace towards others.

We all have seen those who serve God by serving His people but they err in laying heavy burdens upon His people as a price for their service. Their reward ends right there, receiving or prying it from people.

To be a better people, we must each seek for that song in the night. A song that makes heartfelt meditation on God plausible. And meditation that opens our spiritual view to the things God has diligently laid up as treasures for us. You will discover that God is that Song for you, manifesting Himself with frequencies of words caught up in a tune in your mind.

Arise to a new morning from a night where God has whispered His secrets and direction for the time ahead.

Chapter 15

BELIEVE THE WORKS OF GOD MEDITATION

> I will meditate also upon <u>all Your works</u> and consider <u>all Your [mighty] deeds.</u>
>
> ∞ Psalm 77:12 AMPC ∞

Jesus, rebuking the Pharisees and Sadducees of the 1st century AD, said "Believe the works if you do not want to believe me". His laments on Capernaum and Jerusalem were most sorrowful.

> And you, Capernaum, are you to be lifted up to heaven? You shall be brought down to Hades [the region of the dead]! For if <u>the mighty works done in you</u> had been done in Sodom, it would have continued until today.
>
> ∞ Matthew 11:23 ∞

In Capernaum, Jesus performed many mighty miracles. The big earthquake of AD749 destroyed Capernaum. What remains today are the ruins of it. The cry of Jesus over this city was that if the miracles done in Capernaum were done in Sodom, God would not have destroyed it. In other words, there was potential for people in Sodom to repent and turn from their wickedness if the works of God done in Capernaum were done in Sodom.

The rebuke here is clearly about missing the opportunity to be thankful to God and failing to accept the mighty works done before your eyes.

MEDITATING THROUGH THE BIBLE

> Sing to Him, sing praises to Him; meditate on and talk of all His wondrous works and devoutly praise them!
>
> ∞ Psalm 105:2 AMPC ∞

Notice that the works of God are not something we can choose to ignore. From the beginning, when the earth was an empty void, without form and darkness covering the face of the deep, the Spirit of God began by moving over the cold and foggy surface of the waters. When God opened His mouth and spoke, a creative tapestry of works unfolded, beginning with light and ending with a man standing in a garden and communing with God.

When our earthly bodies, our souls, and spirits were held in the depths of a cold darkness after the fall, His Holy Spirit moved upon us. The entrance of His Spirit brought light and now we have fellowship with God.

> The entrance and unfolding of Your words give light; their unfolding gives understanding (discernment and comprehension) to the simple.
>
> ∞ Psalm 119:130 ∞

When in Genesis 1:3 God said, *"Fiat lux"* and *"there was light,"* God never took the light away again. May you find light in your body, soul, and spirit again as you read this. God's words can be received. Allow God to speak His words over your waters, the depth of your soul, and into your spirit. Do not end with just light *(understanding, clarity, knowledge, wisdom)* but be

BELIEVE THE WORKS OF GOD MEDITATION

renewed to be a person who stands in your given garden fully equipped to tend and keep it.

The scripture aptly records some of the first words uttered by God during creation to be "Let there be light". These words were captured by the atmosphere and brought the light of the sun and other constellations. They have brought the light of life into every person and creature that comes into the world since then.

The easily evident work of God is in every living thing you encounter. It does not matter how much scientific you can try and be but life in any form is a wonder beyond the art of science. To not believe God for this kind of work is the most witless thing a beautiful mind can embrace. Faith believes and God inspires men to search out matters and find how things came to be.

Works of God are numerous and variable by nature. The great people of times past and today have unmeshed great discoveries by meditating on God's works. Research work is better performed and obtains better results when those conducting it take time to meditate on the works of God.

There are some fruits and foods that are rich in antioxidants. These were created to specifically act in concert with our bodies to destroy unstable particles in our bodies and help us heal from ailments. But these rogue and mischievous "unstable ones", known as free radicals, seek to cause havoc to our DNA, cell membranes, and other cellular components. Unstable as they are, the free radicals seek room to attach and stabilize themselves in the invaded bodies but they do so by altering the DNA, cells, and structures of the invaded.

Compare the science of the free radicals and oxidants to Jesus' explanation of unclean spirits wreaking havoc in one's life.

MEDITATING THROUGH THE BIBLE

> When the unclean spirit has gone out of a person, it roams through waterless places in search [of a place] of rest (release, refreshment, ease); and finding none it says, I will go back to my house from which I came.
>
> And when it arrives, it finds [the place] swept and put in order and furnished and decorated.
>
> And it goes and brings other spirits, seven [of them], more evil than itself, and they enter in, settle down, and dwell there; and the last state of that person is worse than the first.
>
> ∞ Luke 11:24-26 ∞

Natural and spiritual self-care requires a continuance and filling up our lives with good so that evil will not find room to squeak its way through. God inhabits our praises. Praising God and His works fills our temple with His glory.

The works of God and good deeds must be things we meditate on. The main reason is to fill our thoughts and our hearts with gratitude and expectation for more of the good and better things we have witnessed. We, in turn, glorify God again.

Notice the scripture particularly points to the works and deeds of God and not the workers and doers of these good deeds. This is mainly so because, at any turn, even well-meaning humans may not act in the best interest of the one who has the most need.

To put it simply, there are no princes or princesses we can put our trust in. My family comes first in consideration of priorities, followed by ministry, and the corporate family alike. This is basic and one should not expect you to abandon your family's needs to fulfill your neighbor's first. Charity

BELIEVE THE WORKS OF GOD MEDITATION

begins at home. Giving should remain our priority and we should not allow greed to be a vice we are caught up in.

> Give, and [gifts] will be given to you; good measure, pressed down, shaken together, and running over, will they pour into [the pouch formed by] the bosom [of your robe and used as a bag]. For with the measure you deal out [with the measure you use when you confer benefits on others], it will be measured back to you.
>
> ∞ Luke 6:38 AMPC ∞

God's mighty deeds are evident in that He gives to us. Jesus, who is the Light of the world, the Wisdom of God, and the Bread of Life is given to us. He came and still comes to His own. If we do not receive Him, the Light of God cannot be in us.

> All things were made through Him, and without Him nothing was made that was made. In Him was life, and the life was the light of men. And the light shines in the darkness, and the darkness did not comprehend it.
>
> ∞ John 1:3-5 NKJV ∞

Meditating on the works of God is meditating on the Light-insight, knowledge, revelation, wisdom, and understanding- all flowing from, the great Fountain of Life, the Creator. Light reveals things to us. It makes plain what is hidden in the deep depths, the darkness, and even on the surface. It brings clarity where confusion once reigned

But notice—we are not speaking here of miracles, signs, and wonders. Some people seek miracles in every place, hoping they will be performed for them or upon them. Others believe in God, and miracles, signs, and wonders follow them naturally. They do not chase these things; their lives simply release them. Then there is a third group—those who do not believe that miracles, signs, and wonders are essential to walking with God.

Can you identify the giver, the receiver, and the one who does not receive among these?

The miracles of God are often hidden in the act of giving. Unless you release what is in your hand, how can you reach out to receive more? God gives to us, and yet He has more stored in the heavenly storehouse from which He continues to pour. So be wise in your giving. Do not impoverish yourself, but give equitably, ensuring that all are sustained. Give according to your capacity—what you can hold, reproduce, and share wisely.

God is not after your storehouse. He was not after the young ruler's storehouse either What He desires is your heart—that you would recognize Him as your treasure, your source, and that you are His workmanship, in whom He delights.

If your giving leaves your heart condemned, what good has it done? Perhaps you withheld your hand—giving sparingly and reluctantly. Or perhaps you gave what you borrowed, with no means to repay—giving beyond your ability. What benefit is there in giving this way, when even your own conscience cannot find peace?

Settle your heart. Meditate upon God's works and mighty deeds. No matter how much you give, or receive, we cannot outgive God. In all that you do, let your works be toward the widow, the orphan, and the oppressed. God's eyes are upon them. If you want God to notice you, take notice of them—and help them along the way.

Chapter 16

YOUR MEDITATION CAN BE SWEET TO GOD

> May my meditation be sweet to Him; as for me, I will rejoice in the Lord.
>
> ∞ Psalm 104:34 ∞

Who does not like sweet things? In all your ways, do not make your meditation a sour experience for God. Neither present your meditation with a culinary blandness. Sweetness emanating from one's meditation is a better flavor for God's taste buds. The Old Testament sacrifices were all mostly done with salt added to them, whether it was a flour or a meat sacrifice.

Notice, I am not speaking about your feelings or attitude about meditation at the presentation time. I am speaking about how God sees your meditation when you use it as a tool for communication with Him. Ever wondered why we should enter His courts with thanksgiving and come to the heavenly gates with praise on our lips and thoughts?

The intonation of "may my meditation" seems to show a hesitance in acknowledging that David's meditation is sweet before God, but this is not the case. This is a more contemplative and hopeful tone from a worshiper whose demeanor is to be joyful in the LORD. We know King David by his dancing, warrior mentality, and his music. It is a soul-searching reflection by King David on his meditation seeking to circumcise his approach to meditation and God.

No one enters the greatest king's presence without praise, honor, and reverence for the tenets and strengths of that king. In that regard, regardless of the situation rather choose to rejoice in the presence of God than be sad, sorrowful or indifferent. God is good and in Him, there is no bad. Why bring that rotten tomato attitude before Him? See good by looking beyond any hopeless or unfortunate status. Desire good.

MEDITATING THROUGH THE BIBLE

It is faith to call the things that are not as if they are. However, it is not faith to state the obvious state of the environment you are in whether bad or good.

> So, she set out and came to the man of God at Mount Carmel. When the man of God saw her afar off, he said to Gehazi his servant, Behold, yonder is that Shunammite. Run to meet her and say, "Is it well with you? Well with your husband? Well with the child?" And she answered, "It is well". When she came to the mountain to the man of God, she clung to his feet. Gehazi came to thrust her away, but the man of God said, "Let her alone, for her soul is bitter and vexed within her, and the Lord has hid it from me and has not told me".
>
> ∞ 2 Kings 4:25-27 ∞

The Shunamite woman approached the prophet through whose ministry she had embraced a son with an emphatic "It is well". Her environment was that she had a dead child, but her confession of faith was "It is well".

There is an approach that guarantees you can never be denied anything before God. Sourness and blandness should not be combined with any sorrow. Sorrow in many forms is not a choice but sourness and blandness are choices we choose to accompany us. These should not be confused to be the same as sorrow.

Sorrow accompanied by unshaken faith that says, "Even now, I know that whatever I ask from God, He will grant it to me" has instant access to God's compassion all the time. Even William Shakespeare spoke of "sweet sorrow" in his writing of the Romeo and Juliet play because the two lovers hoped to meet again.

YOUR MEDITATION CAN BE SWEET TO GOD

If we have a mindset to punish God, judge, or question His host of angels because we are faced with a calamity, we lose the opportunity for quick restoration or a turnaround.

Even in the darkest episode, the temperament of joy triumphs over the darkness in that the throne of God's surrounding atmosphere is one filled with worship and praise and not despair. With God, there is no darkness at all. There is no negativity at all.

Before we blabber our reality in His presence, we should extol His reality and capability. Even when faced with bereavement and sorrow, let us remember that to God, our departed loved one has just transitioned into another dimension. To live again in the same body is as easy as just one breath (from God) coming into that body should God command it. At the end of the age, John saw that even the sea gave up the dead that were accumulated in it.

We do not have to repeat the realities of our circumstances but to always bless the LORD. That which is without breath can no longer utter praise to God. God already knows that. If you want to live life well, seek to please God well. While you are alive, on behalf of the living and the dead utter praise to God. Before you sit in counsel with Him, to highlight what the destroyer has taken, be sweet in your meditation.

Do any among us ever recall a moment where God was cornered or forced into answering a gangster-mentality prayer? It is neither the verbosity nor the virulent nature of a prayer that God honors. But an abiding (dwelling) though broken and a contrite spirit that God has never despised. A persisting and fervent faith does not allow the condition of the environment to dictate what God can or cannot do.

Notice that King David was not worried about whether his life was pleasing to God or not. He already had this confidence as a man whose heart was stuck on pleasing God.

MEDITATING THROUGH THE BIBLE

The worst place to be is where one knows their life is far from pleasing the God they are imploring or meditating about.

Elijah walked pleasing God, and a chariot of fire overtook him. Enoch set us a better example. The book of Enoch is filled with wonder in his descriptions of his visits to the realms of the heavenlies.

> And Enoch walked [in habitual fellowship] with God; and he was not, for God took him [home with Him]
>
> ∞ Genesis 5:24 ∞

Who are you pleasing? Fellowship is a shared experience where two or a group of people have common goals, interests, and sometimes common experiences. Enoch was so in tune with God and the celestial realm to the extent that his fellowship with them was habitual. His life did not exhibit a one-way communication but angels in various hierarchies ministered to him and approached and communed with them.

Chapter 17

SPELL IT OUT MEDITATION

> Then Jesus told them, "I tell you the truth, if you have faith and don't doubt, you can do things like this and much more. You can even say to this mountain, 'May you be lifted and thrown into the sea,' and it will happen.
>
> ∞ Matthew 21:21 ∞

One day, when our son, Munoda, was in 4th grade, we were sitting and having a family Bible study. He said something that astounded us. It completely lit our minds and hearts. He touched on the words spell and spelling in their definition forms to make input into being mindful of what we say or speak out.

I will start by giving you the definitions of spelling as given in the flowing dictionaries quoted here:

> Spelling
> - a statement of the exact meaning of a word, especially in a dictionary
> - an exact statement or description of the nature, scope, or meaning of something.
> - the action or process of defining something
> - the degree of distinctness in the outline of an object, image, or sound, especially of an image in a photograph or on a screen
>
> ∞ Oxford Languages ∞

MEDITATING THROUGH THE BIBLE

Humans have used the word spell and its various forms not just to pick out letters of the alphabet that form words but to emphasize the precise characteristics and extent an event, object, action or word has beyond the normal cognitive dimensions of reason.

The word denotes an intangible realm that can be accessed to act in a certain way by words or actions or the mere existence of an object.

We find there is power behind our words, actions, or objects to incite human reactions spurred by our interpretation of what we will have encountered at that moment.

Unfortunately, and often, most people speak negatively about themselves. And even worse, most people have faith in these negative utterances and are entangled in the craftiness of their own tongues. It is no fun being bewitched by one's own mouth. And what is worse is to be the unreasoning or mindless follower of a leader going nowhere or one you already know will get you in trouble with God and the law.

Take the example of an orator, or a person with a certain charisma. It does not take a miracle once they are in front of a receptive audience to cause a pandemonium in one shape or form.

The act of inciting someone does not require an incision into someone's brain, short-circuiting their critical thinking skills, and causing them to act in a certain way. It is spoken words that have the power to do that and spur actions without cognitive analysis.

Look at God, creating the world as we know it. His Spirit moved on the face of the waters, and He began to speak. Things happened.

Look at all the miracles you know of. Words were mostly spoken more than actions were performed.

SPELL IT OUT MEDITATION

When the word spoken collides with its intended subject, that word manifests as has been declared. This is what we are asked to do if we are to move mountains.

> I tell you, you can pray for anything, and if you believe that you've received it, it will be yours.
>
> ∞ Mark 11:23-24 NLT ∞

Other versions of scripture denote prayer with "say". In other words, if you say, you "spell out". The same case is with prayer, you spell out what you are praying for.

The extension of an intentional declaration is often practiced in the courts of law. You say what you mean, and it will be used to define you and your opinion in litigation. If you look at all the words used here, they have a description and meaning of spelling out. They create a picture, a tapestry, in the mind, of what you are saying.

We know that witches and wizards use incantations. And the believer is scared into tatters because of a witch doctor's words! Like as if the believer has no mouth?

Does the witch doctor who has faith in his words become more powerful than a child of God who has faith in God's words? No. Yet, it is possible for a child of God who is without faith in God and themselves to be powerless. Without faith, you are not pleasing to God, and therefore not in a position to receive anything from God. In that case, you become susceptible to any person's words spoken in their faith of what they have to say or have said about you.

MEDITATING THROUGH THE BIBLE

Jesus' teaching said that if you abide in Him and you allow Him to abide in you, you will be fruitful. A branch cut out from the vine and not planted anywhere is dead from the moment the incision separates it from the roots unless grafted or fed by a different mechanism.

What are you spelling out? Are you pruned right to be able to be fruitful? According to my son, whenever you speak, you are casting spells, whether good or bad, firstly on yourself and others.

The meditation of speaking out, or spelling out, in faith is what we should always be engaged in. A person seeking a solution does not say "It can't" but they say, "There should be a way" and they spur themselves into arriving at "We did it".

When you ask for anything, first see yourself as one who already has it. So, give thanks to God, believe, and see it come to be. If you doubt that you already have it, how can God manifest it for you?

The spell-it-out mediation teaches us that, if I want to see something I need or want, I possess it in my inner man first and speak out what it is in faith.

Abraham embraced a son 25 years before the child was manifested. He believed God and did not shy away from speaking about his faith that he had received a son from God.

If you spell it out that you have received it already, then it manifests for you.

Let me sound some very serious caution here with the support of the teaching of the scriptures when they warn us about our tongue being a powerful element that spells out good or doom into our lives.

For the sake of giving context to the bad that happens when one spells out the wrong kind of words, refer to the following scriptures here: *Proverbs 10:31-32; Psalm 34:12-13; Proverbs 12:18-19; Proverbs 15:4; Proverbs 18:21; Proverbs 21:23; James 1:26; James 3:5-8*

SPELL IT OUT MEDITATION

What we speak with our mouths has the capacity to shorten our lives and make life miserable for us.

There are three most powerful elements of any human being; the tongue, the heart, and the brain. If negativity permeates and finds home in any one of these, their influence on each other can be poisonous not only to the one suffering their stay but they poison anything in the host's environment.

If you happen to have a problem with these three being hijacked, please pray for the wisdom that God gives. Remember how God sees and acts without condemning anyone but offering Himself to be our perfect sacrifice. Be a perfect sacrifice from your heart, mind, and tongue to your spirit and those around you.

Remember if we are thinking and speaking certain words we are engaging in premeditation, present time meditating, and post-meditating.

Speaking to His disciples when asked how many times one should forgive someone, Jesus answered Peter to forgive 490 times (70x7) and not 7 times. Forgiveness is what marks the difference between answered prayers and ones that do not. It separates the children of God from those that pretend to be. It crystalizes peace because one who makes peace has no sword in their mouth nor a blazing fire on their tongue.

Spell out the good. Find ways to disinfect your tongue if you must. As much as it can make a natural mouth stink, so does it make one's life smell like rottenness when uncultured words ooze out.

Chapter 18

MY IDENTITY MEDITATION

> You are the salt of the earth, but if salt has lost its taste (its strength, its quality), how can its saltness be restored? It is not good for anything any longer but to be thrown out and trodden underfoot by men.
>
> ∞ Matthew 5:13 AMPC ∞

Jesus used parables to describe our identity. For the purposes of this book and meditation I am alluding to, I will not so much write on the identity of the non-believer. I believe the knowledge, wisdom, and understanding through the identity meditation described herein, as a believer, will help enlighten one making a clear distinction of the non-believer's identity to the reader.

The parables of the Sower are found in three of the Gospels: Matthew 13:1-23, Matthew 13:24-42, Mark 4:1-20, and Luke 8:4-15. The core message of these parables is to convey deeper truths and principles of the identity of people, God's word, and the Sower.

They also provide a glimpse of the reward and judgment that follow each individual seed's choices including the tares. There is not much spoken of concerning the final reward or judgment of the ground.

Elements of Our Identity

Jesus likened our identity as children of God to these five elements upon the earth:

- Salt
- The good seed sown by the Sower
- The ground (of various character) receiving the seed (word) of the Sower
- The light of the world
- The good fish

Jesus also signaled that there was another seed sown, the tares or darnel, whose destiny is to be harvested, bound, and thrown into the fire. Similarly, the fisherman threw away the bad fish and at the end of the age, the angels will throw the wicked into the blazing furnace (Matthew 13:47-50).

As you reflect on what this means, I would like to highlight that Jesus also likened Himself to at least two of these five elements, mainly seed and light. This is interesting. What Jesus said reinforces the scripture that speaks clearly of our identity with great clarity in this manner:

> Love has been perfected among us in this: that we may have boldness in the day of judgment; <u>because as He is, so are we in this world.</u>
>
> ∞ 1 John 4:17 NKJV ∞

MY IDENTITY MEDITATION

Our identity before God is Jesus Christ's identity!

Jesus testified that He was the light of the world. John, in chapter 1 speaks of Jesus as the true Light that lights every person born into this world. Accepting that Light and receiving what it has accomplished is evidenced by being reborn through and to the will of God.

> When Jesus spoke again to the people, he said, 'I am the light of the world. Whoever follows me will never walk in darkness, but will have the light of life.'"
>
> ∞ John 8:12 NIV ∞

The condition to have access to this light and to not walk in darkness or not live a life whose experience is darkness was to follow Him and receive the Light of Life (John 8:12).

We all know the importance of light for the earth and all its creatures. If the sun is a life-giving light to the earth's habitat, how important is the Light of Life that Jesus says we have if we follow Him and His example? Jesus here is not competing with the sun but is indeed elevating human life beyond a body of flesh and emotions.

Remember John says this Light (Jesus) formed the worlds (universe). Having the Light of Life here means having the source, creative power, knowledge, wisdom, and understanding of life and being one with its identity.

MEDITATING THROUGH THE BIBLE

> "While I am in the world, I am the light of the world."
>
> ∞ John 9:5 NIV ∞

In one of the parables of the Sower, Jesus likened us, the children of the Kingdom, to the good seed. Notice the ones who sowed the seed in the parables. Good seed is sown by the Son of man, the term describing Jesus' ministry, as The Prophet, upon the earth.

Both parables in Gospel according Matthew's account show the seed as the people of the kingdom.

> He answered, "The one who sowed the good seed is the Son of Man. The field is the world, and the good seed stands for the people of the kingdom. The weeds are the people of the evil one, and the enemy who sows them is the devil. The harvest is the end of the age, and the harvesters are angels.
>
> ∞ Matthew 13:37-39 NIV ∞

In the book of Matthew, the seed is tied and defined together with the ground upon which it fell. This is ominous in the sense that the wayside, the stony ground, and the thorny ground seed die without multiplication having been affected by the environment.

MY IDENTITY MEDITATION

> But as for the seed sown on good soil, this is the person who hears the word and understands. He bears fruit, yielding a hundred, sixty, or thirty times what was sown.
>
> ∞ Matthew 13:23 NET ∞

But the book of Luke makes a different distinction in defining the identity of the seed. It seemingly adds another parable on the identity of the seed. Though calling the seed the word of God, in expounding on the seed, it makes a distinction similar to the other gospels in that it is talking about people who have had the capacity to hear the Word of God planted in them.

> Now the parable is this: The seed is the word of God.
>
> ∞ Luke 8:11 KJV ∞

How to Maintain the Unchanging Nature of Our Identity

All these elements used to give a believer's identity have a profound character of being powerful and cannot be easily changed in their characteristic identities. Our identity before God is forever settled. We are created in His image with a five-fold blessing (Fruitfulness, Multiplication, Subdue, Replenish, and Dominion) to reveal what He has desired (Genesis 1:28).

- To change salt, it will take some chemical reaction of some sort or dilution.

- To change or alter a seed, one cannot do it unless you alter its DNA.

- To change light, you would need to bleed the power of the source of that light until there is no light to emit and darkness prevails.

- To change the Word of God, it has to be God changing His mind about His Word.

We can manipulate the tangible things and make a hybrid out of them but the life in the seed or the light in it cannot be altered.

In Jesus's admonition about salt losing its flavor, He asked what good is salt that is no longer what it's supposed to be. Can you salt the salt again? The most common way to tamper with salt is to add something to it that it is not. Be careful what you add to yourself or allow others to add into your life. Season your environment well rather than have the environment mangle your identity.

Jesus is the Light that lit our light as we came into this world.

Meditate on the most powerful things we can understand from Jesus' teachings about our identity here:

1. Realize that Jesus positionally placed us into our origin.

2. We are in God.

3. His life, light, strength, taste, savor, creative power, indefectibility, and fruitfulness are already in us.

MY IDENTITY MEDITATION

Environmental Impact on Identity

These are the things Jesus pointed out about us. The big hindrance to this identity flourishing pointed out by Jesus is the environment. In our scientifically advanced time, the environmental aspect that can alter an identity now extends to the DNA of that identity being tampered with.

Take John the Baptist's example, saying he was not that LIGHT. He pointed to that LIGHT. If he had pointed to himself, imagine what that could have been to the disciples who had followed him. They would have missed Jesus, the Seed, the Light, the Salt, the Child of God, and the Word of God who was in their midst. Our witness needs to be a true witness.

Jesus excoriated the Jewish leaders of His time who tried to run the *"we are Abraham's seed"* mantra while condemning Him. Loving Jesus, His teaching and His life is clear evidence that we are children of God (John 8:42).

Who was Jesus then and now? The manifested promise of God. The Seed of the woman. The Word of God sublime. The Light of Life. God inhabiting an earthly body of a human. Is He the same, yesterday, today and forever? He sure is. Are you at peace with all His children? Not being at peace with His children makes it clear you are no child of God (Matthew 5:9).

> I will meditate on Your precepts and have respect for Your ways [the paths of life marked out by Your law].
>
> ∞ Psalm 119:15 AMPC ∞

MEDITATING THROUGH THE BIBLE

The principles (laws) of God require our allegiance to them and their ways. If we take the precept upon precept and the line upon line to meditate therein, we can find our identity and strengthen ourselves to stand in it.

If you cover the light with an obscure object, you can render its capacity to illuminate and remove darkness from around its immediate vicinity weaker than it actually is. In the end, though the light is present, it is not flourishing.

This behooves every one of us to set our light in the open top like a city on a hill.

> You are the light of the world. A city on a hill cannot be hidden. Neither do people light a lamp and put it under a basket. Instead, they set it on a stand, and it gives light to everyone in the house. In the same way, let your light shine before men, that they may see your good deeds and glorify your Father in heaven.
>
> ∞ Matthew 5:14-15 BSB ∞

- Put your light (knowledge, revelation, warmth, life-giving abilities) on a standing place that gives you an advantage against the terrain of life's environment.

- God says I am all that He envisioned me to be. My light should not be diminished by anything.

- I am a well-seasoning salt. I am not saltless nor unworthy. I cannot be thrown out to trampled on.

- I am not a seed fallen on the wayside, stony ground or the thorny field.

MY IDENTITY MEDITATION

- I am not a hard earth that cannot nurture God's Word well.

- I have not set myself in an environment thorny and choking the light.

- I am a cultivated earth. I have cultivated, aerated my heart, and made it arable to bear God more seed.

- I am not someone other than what God's Word is about me.

What is your identity? What is your meditation about yourself?

Chapter 19

∞

STILLNESS MEDITATION

> "Be still and know that I am God; I will be exalted among the nations, I will be exalted over the earth.
>
> ∞ Psalm 46:10 BSB ∞

What thoughts were on God's mind when He took a clod of dirt and began to fashion Adam? What thoughts of God were transposed into Adam as God went about creating him?

Have you ever been still before God? How about being quiet before God? Have you ever spent time alone with God? Do you have an idea how all this relates to your well-being? Have you come to know who God is by delving into the stillness that reveals from it who He is?

Most worshippers do not even know how to be still, let alone be quiet. We struggle to still our minds in life most of the time. We are busier in our minds figuring out how to pay the next bill than we are inclined to be still.

Should we find ourselves alone, we are drawn to virtual worlds through digital devices and we land right in the middle of other people's business. The thoughts and thirsts that have the biggest bark are what we utter and feed.

We are always in constant need of company, dreading to be alone. This is not a bad desire at all but overindulgence in it to the point you do not have your own time of solitude leaves one no room to self and God.

Yet the best way to never be alone is to know how to be still and be in the company of God and His angels.

Abram had kept in his company his nephew Lot. Traveling from Mesopotamia into Canaan with the promise of God before Him, things looked good. He had fellowship with his troupe and Lot helped him along the journey.

But there is a mysterious gap in how many times God appeared to Him and how many times he built an altar to worship God. At the first altar, God spoke to him saying he would give the land of Canaan as an inheritance to his children. Abram's second altar in his travel east of Bethel is recorded without an appearance of God.

After this second altar, Abram's life seemed so busy and had famine-related migration into Egypt. He even conspired with Sarai and gave her away as wife to Pharaoh fearing for his life. Had it not been God intervening and mysteriously stopping Pharaoh, his history could have been very different.

Coming back into Canaan, he came to the place of his second altar east of Bethel and worshipped God again. By this time, even though coming out from a recent famine, he was loaded. And so too was his nephew, Lot. And with the wealth came a lot of noise and eventual separation from Lot.

> The Lord said to Abram after Lot had left him, Lift up now your eyes and look from the place where you are, northward and southward and eastward and westward; For all the land which you see I will give to you and to your posterity forever.
>
> ∞ Genesis 13:14-15 AMPC ∞

Notice the significance of when God speaks to Abram in Genesis 12th and 13th chapters. God speaks to him when he arrives in Canaan, at the first altar but does not do so again until Lot had left him.

STILLNESS MEDITATION

Reading between the lines, one can see that the second altar did not yield fellowship with God the first two times Abram is mentioned calling on the name of the LORD until Lot had left. One can infer that it was not Abram's return from Egypt but Lot's separation from Abram that opened an opportunity for the man to hear God speak to him again.

One might ask what this has to do with stillness and with meditation. Have you ever found yourself so busy with your job, business, or other people's business that you do not find time to stop and find yourself again?

In the hustle, tussle, and bustle of life meditation moments become a casualty and may seem like a luxury. There is just not enough space to be quiet, alone, and still.

Where there is no stillness, there is no quiet. And we miss God and the victory and blessing He confers in the stillness. It is not the famine that moves God to speak and act on our behalf. How and when we pay attention to Him is key. Even in the midst of a battle we must learn to fight while quietly waiting before God for His inspiration.

> I wait quietly before God, for my victory comes from Him.
>
> ∞ Psalm 62:1 NLT ∞

Lot was a prince even when he was with Abram. He did not find it strange to speak against his uncle, especially after their adventure into Egypt brought them a lot of riches. After all, this childless uncle Abram with his barren wife did not have him in the long-term picture to inherit their estate. They were fixated on a promise of a son that was long in coming.

It is not only King David who faced this in life but Abram had a taste of this early on.

> Princes also did sit and speak against me: but thy servant did meditate in thy statutes.
>
> ∞ Psalm 119:23 KJV ∞

It takes virtue to hold your peace amid a tumult and revolt against you. A great example is King David and the story in 2 Samuel 16. Shimei reveled in mockery on the hillside to the extent of spitting on the ground David walked.

A Still Small Voice in the Stillness

1 Kings 19 tells the story of a prophet fleeing the threat of death from Jezebel. Elijah was woken up by an angel twice from a hungry and tired sleep to be given food to eat when hiding in the wilderness before he escaped to Mount Horeb.

When in a cave around Mount Horeb, God asked him what he was up to. Having felt dejected and wanting to die after Jezebel's threat, he felt helpless.

STILLNESS MEDITATION

> Then the LORD said, "Go out and stand on the mountain before the LORD. Behold, the LORD is about to pass by."
>
> And a great and mighty wind tore into the mountains and shattered the rocks before the LORD, but the LORD was not in the wind. After the wind there was an earthquake, but the LORD was not in the earthquake. After the earthquake there was a fire, but the LORD was not in the fire. And after the fire came a still, small voice. When Elijah heard it, he wrapped his face in his cloak and went out and stood at the mouth of the cave. Suddenly a voice came to him and said, "What are you doing here, Elijah?"
>
> ∞ 1 Kings 19:11-13 BSB ∞

God disrupted Elijah's kind of quietness and stillness built on fear and lethargy.

He told him to stand upon the mount and witness the acts of God's power and presence. The wind, earthquake, and fire may accompany God's move, but they are not to be mistaken with His voice. Sometimes, it takes hearing beyond the noise, being still enough to discern the silence to hear God's voice in the stillness.

A display of God's power is not the same as the voice of God. God can demonstrate His power by creating something out of nothing or utilizing the elements we can see. Using elements and individuals that can work good or bad, God can show His hand but His essence is revealed in peace.

So, possess yourself in peace and patience amidst all the hustle, tussle, and bustle. Find in yourself a quiet, still secret place to dwell and commune with God and yourself. Make better company by yourself with God and self in the stillness.

MEDITATING THROUGH THE BIBLE

And the angel of the LORD called unto Abraham out of heaven the second time, And said, By myself have I sworn, saith the LORD, for because thou hast done this thing, and hast not withheld thy son, thine only son: That in blessing I will bless thee, and in multiplying I will multiply thy seed as the stars of the heaven, and as the sand which is upon the sea shore; and thy seed shall possess the gate of his enemies; And in thy seed shall all the nations of the earth be blessed; because thou hast obeyed my voice.

∞ Genesis 22:15-18 ∞

Chapter 20

TRUST MEDITATION

> Trust in the LORD always, for the LORD GOD is the eternal Rock.
>
> ∞ Isaiah 26:4 ∞

David sums up his trust by saying, *"Some trust in chariots and others in horses, but we trust in the name of the LORD our God"* (Psalm 20:7)

There is no doubt that we should trust in God. It is a fundamental principle that, if you have a good relationship with someone, it is easy to establish trust. Where there is a bad or non-existent relationship, trust is naturally eroded or extinct. Trust requires the symbiosis of a mutual environment for the two entities engaging in it.

What is trust? What is its relationship with my beliefs, character, expectations, and behavior? When it comes to trust, do I have to do anything to establish it as an expectation to and from others? Can it be won? Can it be rebuilt where it has been damaged? What is trust's relationship with beliefs or faith? What is your trust based on? All these questions do not have a single answer.

Trust depends on the context it is defined for in the relationship. Trust is expected from and towards the object or relationship in which it is given. One cannot build trust where reliability, integrity, and consistent behavior are missing in action unless that trust is blind. Yet trust is not blind to the values that define it. When you do away with defining values of trust, your walk together has no direction, purpose, or communion, and it is worthless.

> Do two walk together except they make an appointment and have agreed?
>
> ∞ Amos 3:3 AMPC ∞

MEDITATING THROUGH THE BIBLE

With blind trust, one can evade conflict and strife but even God will not have blind trust in anything or anyone. The Bible teaches us to never put our trust in anyone, not even princes or potentates.

> It is better to trust in the LORD than to put confidence in man.
> It is better to trust in the LORD than to put confidence in princes.
>
> ∞ Psalm 118:8-9 KJV ∞

Blind trust is subject to abuse in that the trustor gives up on examining the quality of the trustee and leaves everything at the mercy and goodwill of the trustee. With human-to-human trust, this is an obvious pitfall. It was a pitfall even between humans and the watcher angels in the day of Noah leading to a near-human wipe-out deluge.

Let's go back a little to basics. Faith, belief, and trust have interconnected contexts, but they are very different. Trust is evidence and experience driven. Belief is an acceptance of some truth or existence of something with or without the requirement to prove it.

Faith is a deeper conviction of trust and belief, not requiring visible or tangible proof. Faith is celestial and incomprehensible in that it extends beyond the observable and measurable qualities. With faith, you consider that the things you seek have already been provided.

Notice, that faith is not blind to present reality. It merely seeks and leans on a better yet unseen reality. If all we see is the only things that are real, then there is no reasonable ground for faith. We know there is more to what is unseen, hence we all have faith, in one form or another.

TRUST MEDITATION

Trust, by definition, is confidence or reliance on the quality of someone or something one has that trust in. We trust because we have confidence in the certainty of the character, truth, ability, or strength of the individual or subject we have such a feeling and decision to bestow such trust. In other words, trust is quality centered.

Trust is knowledge-based. If you know the quality of your God, you have no problems trusting that God. If you do not know the quality, then you have blind trust.

Belief on the other hand is an acceptance of a notion that something is true or exists. Belief can be evidence-based where factual information exists or can be based on theories, opinions, and experimental conclusions limited to a particular sampling.

A striking example is the long-standing belief that the Earth was flat, which led to the persecution of those who provided empirical evidence proving it was a sphere.

> Let not your heart be troubled: ye believe in God, believe also in me.
>
> ∞ John 14:1 KJV ∞

Jesus insinuated that His disciples, and indeed most of humanity, trust in God. If you believe in Jesus, trust Him. The Greek word, *pisteuó*, used in this verse, and the early Aramaic word, *haymnu*, both mean to believe or to trust.

In writing this chapter, I strongly felt the need to not only reflect on trust in God as a form of meditation, but also to broaden the scope to include trust in all types of relationships.

MEDITATING THROUGH THE BIBLE

This approach is important because I aim to clarify and distinguish between trust, faith, and belief—three concepts that are often misunderstood or misapplied spiritually and secularly.

Many of life's challenges stem from misplaced trust, misguided faith, or unfounded belief. Without a solid understanding of these foundational principles, we often find ourselves hurt, confused, and emotionally depleted.

Too often, we place trust in our enemies, families, and governments without reason or discernment. Even in abusive relationships—where the very definition of the relationship is unclear, unacknowledged, or spiritually and emotionally harmful—we still find ourselves clinging to a form of "trust" rooted in blind faith.

This kind of trust becomes circular: a "trust in trust" or "faith in faith," where the foundational trust or faith doesn't truly exist. It's a misplaced reliance, built not on reality or mutual respect, but on a hope that lacks substance and a fate resigned to end in failure.

We don't trust in God because our faith and belief processes are messed up. We think, feel, talk, and act like we have God and His host of angels as our errands team. We unintelligently question God and reduce Him and His angels to puppets.

Are you someone whose prayers seem to go unanswered? Take a moment to reflect on how you truly revere God—there, you may begin to uncover the reason.

Do you appear to have it all, yet feel spiritually blind, broken, exposed, and burdened?

It may be time to reexamine and realign your trust, faith, and belief—both in God and in yourself—through intentional meditation, until they are rooted in God's perspective.

TRUST MEDITATION

Only then can healing, clarity, and true spiritual fulfillment begin.

Trust does not mean inaction to and from the parties involved in its exchange. Trust should be cultivated in as much as faith and belief should be.

Trust meditation can be very fruitful if engaged in meaningfully from many angles:

- Start by having meditations on weaning yourself from trusting man, institutions, and your own understanding.

- To truly benefit from the practice of trust meditation, follow through by releasing relationships that lack mutual trust or reciprocity. Sometimes, the most powerful act of trust is choosing to step back from connections that keep you BUSY—Being Under Someone's Yoke. Letting go isn't a weakness; it's wisdom. It's the recognition that trust, to be transformative, must be shared, not one-sided.

- Learn to horn in your faith, belief, and trust in God. We receive from the unseen because we have faith, and we please God by our faith.

We are all born with an innate desire and inclination to trust. This is good if we follow through to ensure that we have acquired the value needed to transact trust. Otherwise, the desire to trust is a huge vulnerability that those around you who are cunning can exploit. The greatest betrayal is one carried out by the person you keep close to who, once before, has taken the bullet intended for you in the past.

When trust is absent or blind, one is bound to grow cold in their relationship with God. Such is the Laodicean condition, of trusting in self, miscalculating one's wealth, and dismissing one's need for the Divine One in their life. (Reference Revelation chapter 3). Notice, that Jesus was already outside of this relationship. He was standing at the door and knocking to be let in.

In your relationship, are you dwelling on the inside, or you have been unceremoniously left in the cold or the heat of the outside? Where do you have God abiding trust wise and in His person?

Remember trust can be built upon from one glory to another till it is solid and unshaken like the sacred hills.

Having laid a good foundation for understanding why trust meditation is a good and needed practice, let us conclude this subject matter well.

Do you trust God enough? How does your meditation of trusting Him stack up?

Can God trust you? Like He trusted Enoch? Abraham? Moses? Job? Mary? Is there a value and quality system on you that testifies on your behalf? What is stopping you from building it if it is lacking?

Did you know that true meditation begins with trust?

To meditate meaningfully, you must trust both the process and the One to whom your meditation is directed.

You must also believe in—and trust—the unique gift and calling placed upon your life. Without that foundation, meditation becomes just another routine, rather than a transformative spiritual practice.

> Meditate on these things; give yourself entirely to them, so that your progress may be evident to all.
>
> ∞ 1 Timothy 4:15 NKJV ∞

TRUST MEDITATION

You cannot meditate on a prophecy you do not believe in. Did Joshua have a prophecy? King David? Jesus? Do you have a prophecy? Genesis 1:28, Matt 11:28, Jeremiah 33:3

Chapter 21

COMMUNION & REMEMBRANCE MEDITATION

> He took some bread and gave thanks to God for it. Then he broke it in pieces and gave it to the disciples, saying, "This is my body, which is given for you. Do this in remembrance of me."
>
> ∞ Luke 22:19 NLT ∞

One of the most vivid teachings of Christ Jesus was the *Eucharist*. In this teaching and ritual, Jesus points to broken bread as His body. He still had His physical body, in which His Spirit dwelt, yet He projected His body onto the bread He took and broke after giving thanks.

The word *Eucharist is a Greek word* meaning *"thanksgiving", "gratitude"* or to *show favor very well or giving grace.*

In essence, communion requires that we are fully aware of the body broken for us and that we are thankful for it to God. Favor has been given to us in that we have received the sacrifice of His body. Beyond favor, God has extended to us grace beyond any level of deserving such grace.

If then we have received His body, broken sufficiently for us to manifest His favor, we have also received His Spirit. While His body is given for sacrifice, His Spirit is given for life and for intercession to do away with any condition that separates us from the Father.

This is the full essence of the Eucharist. When you take the bread, see the body of Christ, broken, in full sufficiency, for you and against every negative condition that opposes His magnanimity on you and beyond you. We have received from God through Jesus' sacrifice the capstone of grace (Zechariah 4:7).

If Jesus had, in some way, shape, or form torn his own body to pieces and given His disciples to eat His flesh while asking them to be thankful to God

MEDITATING THROUGH THE BIBLE

and to remember Him, what would we all have thought? In full disclosure, if I think I am my own body, I can only see cannibalistic inclinations from this instruction from Jesus.

But here Jesus pointing to bread was not imposing importance to an earthly bread, human flesh nor did He point towards His earthly body. See the symbolism He was applying in this text.

> He who takes my flesh for food and my blood for drink is in me and I in him. As the living Father has sent me, and I have life because of the Father, even so, <u>he who takes me for his food will have life because of me.</u> This is the bread which has come down from heaven. It is not like the food which your fathers had: they took of the manna, and are dead, but he who takes this bread for food will have life forever.
>
> ∞ John 6:56-58 KJV ∞

Jesus said He is the eternal life-giving bread that came down from heaven. As the last Adam, He is a life-giving Spirit. What body do you give a spirit except the one it chooses to attach to? Remember *He was crucified before the foundations of the world (Rev13:8)*.

If you look closely at John 6, you will realize Jesus says *the body of flesh is not profitable, but the spirit is life-giving.* The most powerful thing about Him is that His words were spirit and life just like He said. Communion or the Eucharist taken in meditation opens a plateau of treasures in the form of God's words, life-giving, and powerful to make everything new again.

COMMUNION & REMEMBRANCE MEDITATION

When we engage in remembrance of Jesus, it is not only mainly for His earthly body's remembrance but more so for the teaching and sayings He espoused and hence the spirit and life that they are to us.

We receive the bread and the cup from His Spirit to our spirit and give it preeminence within our earthly body, spirit, and our environment. This is how we become the manifested body of His Spirit and have the Holy Spirit abiding in us to continue His works. And we also, as branches abide in the vine bearing much fruit to the glory of God and our individual and collective benefit.

More than anything else in the walk of life, hearing God speak to oneself is most precious. His words are life and the very things we desire are ready to be spoken into existence at the breath of His voice if we indeed can believe Him, be still, and listen.

The problem is that throughout our generations, we hear and fear the thundering around us more than we tune ourselves to the still small voice beyond the bluster of the noise.

We lose the opportunity to hear God by what we choose to listen to and pay attention to. *"Whoever has (spiritual) ears, let them hear what the Spirit says..." (Revelation 2:29).* To hear the Spirit, one must have the hearing qualities upon which the Spirit's voice can be deciphered. There are many sound frequencies out there but it takes a special eardrum and exposure to decode a frequency that is special and rare.

One of the greatest hindrances to hearing God's voice is the convergence of distorted religion, corrupt politics, and restrictive or liberal traditions. Unfortunately, in some instances entire nations and cultures become trapped in man-made spiritual prisons—places where intimate fellowship with God is silenced or altogether absent.

MEDITATING THROUGH THE BIBLE

These prisons often are created by perceived spiritual prelates who seek more personal glory and control of the people than they seek for God to be known by the people they lead. The result always leaves nations or certain groups of people decimated and having to rebuild again. Beyond corporate worship seek the voice of God and one-on-one fellowship with Him more.

True spirituality or religion should elevate its participants into supernal beings—loving, enlightened, and fully alive as children of God. Yet when self-serving spiritual leaders rise, they become principalities of hindrance, cloaking their ambition in seductive doctrines that serve their own agendas.

These spiritual gatekeepers have no qualms about advancing systems that make us subservient to their intellect, authority, and limitations—while they quietly drain the fruit of our minds, our labor, and our strength. These serpents beguile us taking what was ours while giving us sweat and death.

Have you ever wondered why Adam and Eve only began to sweat and feel the toll of their work on their bodies after the fall? A break in communion with God precipitated this. What would a continual communion with God do to you? What are the possibilities of success when you live in remembrance of the LORD to the point you can hear His silent whisper?

Have you ever realized that in Jesus asking us to remember Him, He was pointing us to remember who we are in relation to Him and God's original intent?

Envision your body as a similar bread to the one Jesus envisioned His body as. Envision your blood as a similar drink to His own blood. Would God take your body as bread and your blood as drink and give it for the life of the world? Can He trust the current inclination of the imagination of your heart to save the world?

Chances are you disqualify yourself based on what you have done in the past, even when forgiven of it. God has not asked us to sacrifice ourselves

COMMUNION & REMEMBRANCE MEDITATION

this way but to let go of an identity that feels disqualified to accept His sacrifice.

Humans and animals alike may sacrifice their lives for the sake of their children but not for strangers or non-family individuals. To Jesus, we are already family regardless of our sin condition, because His sacrifice is enough. We can never outgive Him but that does not mean we should then be selfish.

When taking communion or meditating, believe that God is well pleased to dwell with you and within. There is no reason to not believe so. He was well pleased with Jesus. You are feasting on the body God was well pleased with and have become what you eat.

Would Jesus have asked us to eat of His flesh and drink His blood if we did not have need of doing it? Why is such a transposition or transubstantiation of flesh to bread and blood to a cup of wine or vice versa critical? Is the imagination of it as the body and blood of Jesus more important than the faith and living transformation that one who practices the communion or Eucharist should show? What do you think and how is your faith shaped concerning this remembrance act?

Before being driven from the Garden of Eden after the fall, Adam and Eve were covered by God with animal skin *(signifying Jesus covering humanity with His own flesh and blood)*. This is significant. For people into whom sin had made an entrance, God restored their capacity to stand before Him, with sin not becoming a separator, by the covering of innocent flesh and blood.

Unlike Cain who walked away from the presence of God sad and fallen, Adam and Eve were sent away from Eden but never from the presence of God.

I call to your memory that in the Lord's Prayer (Matthew 6:9-13), Jesus teaches us to place a demand for our daily bread before God. God is Spirit and humans have a dual nature (flesh and spirit).

MEDITATING THROUGH THE BIBLE

Preceding the prayer, Jesus says we should not worry or come before God seeking what we shall eat, drink, or wear. It clearly follows that the bread Jesus teaches us to place a demand for is more than wheat, rice, corn or rye flour-based bread.

> But He answered and said, "It is written, Man shall not live by bread alone, but by every word that proceeds from the mouth of God.'"
>
> ∞ Matthew 4:4 NKJV ∞

I need not expound on the cup that signifies His blood shed for us. Clearly, when making a covenant or reinforcing one, you signify it by an act, the more prophetic the better, to be binding and worthy of the promise or agreement it is based on. Jesus made a covenant with us based on His own life *(life is in the blood of a living flesh)*.

We examine ourselves by meditating and taking stock of our intention in the covenant we have with Him during communion. To do otherwise, and not to meditate and believe in the communion, is to disregard the covenant.

Chapter 22

FALL IN LOVE WITH PRECEPT MEDITATION

> Make me understand the way of Your precepts; so, shall I meditate on and talk of Your wondrous works.
>
> ∞ Psalm 119:27 ∞

Psalm Chapter 119 is the chapter with the most verses on meditation. Most of them cover precept meditation.

A precept is meant to help and aid us in regulating how we conduct ourselves. It is intended to help guide our proclivities, intentions, and behaviors.

This means, in essence, we can meditate on precept before we engage into our proclivities, intentions, and behaviors to better guide ourselves into the best of outcomes. Imagine if we could intercept every harmful impulse, every wandering thought, and anchor our intentions on the elevated plane of goodness. Would you resist such a noble aspiration of the heart?

Would it not be nice to read about Noah's time differently with the verse saying, "The Lord saw that the wickedness of man was greatly diminished in the earth, and that every imagination and intention of all human thinking was only non-evil continually"? That generation would have made God so pleased if it did that.

Notice that the antidote to wickedness begins with a pure intention and a clean imagination. Beware the subtle seed of envy and the quiet harboring of wounded pride—they are early warning signs of uncontrollable anger. When Cain became entangled in this volatile mix of emotions, the spirit of murder reshaped his legacy. It never left Cain with room for remorse or repentance, driving away captive from the presence of God.

MEDITATING THROUGH THE BIBLE

A precept extends beyond the letter of the law or commandment and is based on moral or spiritual guidance. It speaks to the spirit or the core of a person. On the other hand, a law on the same issue mandates or prohibits certain actions accompanied by legal consequences for violations. God's precept gives life while a law on the same issue seeks to protect life from being violated.

Open your heart to understand even the scriptures that condemn your most cherished or most excused propensities. Why would God make some noise about something if there is no harm to me and you emanating from it? So even the precept of God that speaks against your corruption must be celebrated by you?

> My hands also will I lift [in fervent supplication] to Your commandments, which I love, and I will meditate on Your statutes.
>
> ∞ Psalm 119:48 AMPC ∞

The key to the victory of Jesus against Satan, when tempted in the wilderness after 40 days of fasting, was the precept. There was no law against Jesus turning stones into bread when He was hungry. There was a precept for a man (Jesus was a man in this instance) to not live by bread alone. Deuteronomy 8:3.

Examine the things you are so much against that God is not against during your meditation. Examine God's precepts. Seating from God's vantage point examine your bias, intentions, and behaviors. What about envy, wounded pride, and anger? The precept helps you keep from derailing your life, peace and the love of God.

FALL IN LOVE WITH PRECEPT MEDITATION

Why allow your heart to condemn you for tendencies you already know lean toward evil? Does stepping away from your weaknesses, fears, and the weight of condemnation truly leave you at an eternal disadvantage? How? Humble your pride before it humiliates you—better to surrender it than to be disgraced by it.

> Let the proud be put to shame, for they dealt perversely with me without a cause; but I will meditate on Your precepts.
>
> ∞ Psalm 119:78 AMPC ∞

King David, in his repentance, chose to let his sin be what it was, his sin. His sin was not him. Because of sin, God cursed the ground and not humanity. We should desist from kicking ourselves further deep down into the mire when we fail or sin. Neither should we fail to love the law. Jesus came not for its abolishment but to fulfill it by living above its requirements.

> Oh, how love I Your law! It is my meditation all the day.
>
> ∞ Psalm 119:97 AMPC ∞

Rather than be found hating the scales of justice, fall in love with the precepts of God to the extent of meditating on them. The excellency of departing from running on evil is that life is poured out to those whose reverence of God propels them to eschew evil. Solomon equates both wisdom and money to a defense that protects the life of the one who has it. To know such wisdom, to be that rich, Solomon meditated well and knew what to ask God for in his encounter with God.

MEDITATING THROUGH THE BIBLE

> Wisdom is as good as an inheritance, yes, more excellent it is for those [the living] who see the sun. For wisdom is a defense even as money is a defense, but the excellency of knowledge is that wisdom shields and preserves the life of him who has it.
>
> ∞ Ecclesiastes 7:11-12 AMPC ∞

Solomon and Job teach wisdom as the fear or reverence of God in a person. They regard knowledge as the capacity to run away from evil. To properly understand and meditate on precept, I recommend additional reading, study, and meditation on Job Chapter 28 and Proverbs Chapter 8.

When it comes to God's precepts, there is an important caveat we must all recognize: we often seek understanding, yet His ways may not always make immediate sense to us. Rather than striving solely to grasp every precept, let your greater pursuit be to hold tightly to God's hand. As you walk with Him in trust and closeness, understanding will come— maybe not all at once, but steadily, as He leads you step by step, "precept upon precept two-fold; line upon line two-fold. Here a little and there a little". Isaiah 28:10.

Chapter 23

MEDITATION ON GOD'S TESTIMONIES

> I have a better understanding and deeper insight than all my teachers because Your testimonies are my meditation.
>
> ∞ Psalm 119:99 AMPC ∞

If King David had a teacher in his time, that teacher would have surely been proud of his accomplishments. But if the teacher had been a destiny thief, he might have scoffed and said, "You're too proud." The truth is, a great teacher opens doors wider than their own—for students to rise, excel, and even surpass them. Such a teacher is truly golden. Golden teachers do not have a problem with the verse above.

Anyone, teacher or fellow student who deliberately narrows the path for another to excel is, in essence, a thief of destiny. Words, reactions, and even silent thoughts can carry a limiting force—and when expressed, they can build invisible walls that hinder someone's progress. This is especially damaging when the person harboring such limiting intentions holds influence over the other's future.

In this verse, King David was still referencing the precepts of God. He gives context as to how his diligence in observing the precepts of God had opened his wisdom and understanding to flow at higher levels.

We know that a testimony is a formal spoken or written statement with a standing in a court of law. It stands as a witness or proof provided by the declaration of firsthand experience of something. A testimony is a manifestation of something verified by someone.

MEDITATING THROUGH THE BIBLE

In the temple blueprint as given by God to Moshe:

- The Ark of the Covenant housing the two tablets of the Ten Commandments,

- The table with the shewbread,

- And the seven golden wicks branched candelabra

All stood as the witness (testimony) that indeed God was among them. The two tablet stones of the law were referred to as the testimony, while the Menorah or candelabra (the seven-wick golden lampstand) symbolized the Eternal Light and the illumination of God to His people. The shewbread stood as a testimony of God's provision to Israel.

Imagine how King David meditated on God's testimonies. He had come to a level of insight by meditation where he loved the law. The convergence of observing the law and God's precepts led him to see God's testimonies. If a testimony is God's, who can argue against it? The witness and declaration of God simply put is better than gold or even life itself. Nothing can equal it. You can richly bank on God's testament.

> To the law and to the testimony: if they speak not according to this word, it is because there is no light in them.
>
> ∞ Isaiah 8:20 KJV ∞

The importance of God's testimony is so paramount. It divides between those who have no light and the ones who have. Study and meditate to understand, like David, the meaning of the temple elements I mentioned

MEDITATION ON GOD'S TESTIMONIES

here. Now looking at Isaiah chapter 8:20 do you see how the light represents precept?

Having this Light in you precipitates an inclination towards the law and testimonies of God. It is a precept, a guiding beacon. The clear safe and sound choice in life is to choose the light, to be in it, and to be a derivative of it.

> So I fell at his feet to worship him. But he told me, "Do not do that! I am a fellow servant with you and your brothers who rely on the testimony of Jesus. Worship God! For the testimony of Jesus is the spirit of prophecy."
>
> ∞ Revelation 19:10 BSB ∞

The declaration of God Himself among us, revealing Himself, is a testimony and the full extent of the law in manifestation. This means the law and the testimony of God are active, alive, and powerful by their nature, as God is because they carry a part of His essence. The blessing of His person when He has made His abode amongst us and within is palpable.

In Deuteronomy 29:5, the soles of shoes refused to wear out through common use when the children of Israel dwelt under the pillar of fire by night and His cloud by day in the wilderness. Imagine a pair of shoes whose soles do not wear out for over 40 years.

The phrase *"the testimony of Jesus is the Spirit of prophecy"* is spoken by an angel (a messenger and a spiritual entity not subject to human limitations). This profound statement helps us understand Isaiah's words better.

MEDITATING THROUGH THE BIBLE

From Isaiah 9:6, John chapters 1, 14, and 17, and Colossians chapters 1 and 2, we gain a profound understanding of the identity of Jesus—the Christ of God. His testimony is inseparable from the testimony of God, and at the heart of this testimony lies the Spirit of prophecy.

Revelation 19:10 highlights the extraordinary wisdom and knowledge that the Spirit of prophecy can manifest through a servant of God. The revelation was so overwhelming that John, in awe, fell to his knees to worship the prophetic angel. Yet the angel, walking in humility and divine understanding, refused the worship and simply declared, "Worship God."

This response reveals a powerful truth: those who carry the Spirit of prophecy with humility never seek glory for themselves. Their consistent testimony is one of reverence, pointing others back to God. That is the true blessing of the gift—it magnifies God, not the vessel.

> And I am John, who heard and saw these things. And when I had heard and seen them, I fell down to worship at the feet of the angel who had shown me these things. But he said to me, "Do not do that! I am a fellow servant with you and your brothers the prophets, and with those who keep the words of this book. Worship God!"
>
> ∞ Revelation 22:8-9 BSB ∞

Regardless of the gift and calling anyone operates in, one should not receive or accept worship from any person. We should be careful to not fall into this trap of worshipping fellow human beings, angels, or any illustrious ones who God uses mightily. All who lead, inspire, and guide others too should

MEDITATION ON GOD'S TESTIMONIES

be careful to not receive the worship of anyone. God's faithful servants point to Him and not themselves.

There is no light, wisdom, knowledge, understanding, freedom, and faithfulness in the one who receives worship intended for the Creator or the one who points people to any other than the Creator Himself.

Meditate in the Spirit of prophecy and begin to walk in better understanding and deeper perception. The Spirit of prophecy bears witness to Jesus Christ. It validates God's intentions.

> Suppose there are prophets among you or those who dream dreams about the future, and they promise you signs or miracles, 2and the predicted signs or miracles occur. If they then say, 'Come, let us worship other gods'—gods you have not known before— 3do not listen to them. The LORD your God is testing you to see if you truly love him with all your heart and soul.
>
> ∞ Deuteronomy 13:1-3 NLT ∞

Now, if your intention, words, and thoughts are convergent with God's, would what you desire and speak fail to be? The Spirit of prophecy exists not just for prophetic insight but it also validates us if we dwell in Him. It reveals He dwells in us. Only God is the Alpha and the Omega. What is your testimony?

Chapter 24

THE SECRETS OF ENOCH'S WALK WITH GOD

> I remember the days of old; I meditate on all Your doings; I ponder the work of Your hands.
>
> ∞ Psalm 143:5 AMPC ∞

Do you meditate on all of God's doings? Do you meditate on your own doings at all? The second question here is not intended to be minor at all. How can one truthfully search their own heart? It is a fact that King David contemplated all, not some, of all of God's doings. It would be difficult to assume King David did not take stock of his own doings when he meditated on God's manifested acts.

We know of Enoch—the man who walked so closely with God that he entered eternity without tasting death. What were the secrets of his divine walk? Sadly, Enoch's writings were excluded from the canonized Bible by the councils that determined which prophetic and apostolic texts would form the Scriptures we know today.

Isn't there a natural curiosity in all of us to understand what this prophet was truly like? Can we uncover the mysteries he knew—the insights that made him seemingly invincible to the forces that shape ordinary human destiny?

Historical patterns show that humanity often omits the very truths that empower the individual to rise above limitation. Enoch is on record, in his non-canonical writings, claiming to have spent extended time in angelic realms, heavenly dimensions, and even before the throne of God itself.

Such a testimony invites us to wonder: What kind of life must one live to walk in such intimacy with the divine? And what might we learn if we dared to walk as he did?

MEDITATING THROUGH THE BIBLE

It is mainly from the book of Enoch that we know the names of the angels, their hierarchy, and the names of the infamous lustful ones who descended, took human form, made a pact on Mount Hermon, and took wives from the human race. Enoch's book has a lot of striking similarities with those books that give an account of the heavenly realms.

I strongly suggest reading this book. It is available for download on various apps whether for Windows, Android, or Apple devices.

One of the biggest takeaways I have from this book is that a human being is so special before God to the extent that God has set angels as ministering spirits to humanity. God also exercises judgment and punishment against those angels that corrupt humanity.

While all this is true, the anchor in it all is that each human has been endowed with the power of yes or no as an answer to any suggestion, good or bad, coming from whosoever. Our capacity to choose comes with a blessing or curse depending on what we have inclined ourselves to.

What did Enoch choose? How can we find out?

Our modern generations are in full-throttle social media overdrive. People crave salacious stories, snappy one-liners, short-form videos, and fast-paced audio-visual content. Constantly, they're judging, commenting, opining, and tossing around casual "just saying" remarks—whether short or tall tales.

But remember: the last time someone engaged in a sinister "just saying" in heaven, it led to a third of the angels falling from their estate. Worse still, on earth, the Garden of Eden was emptied. Today, this behavior is so common that many no longer have a conscience sharp enough to resist these toxic exchanges—what you might call "soup parties" of gossip and careless speech.

THE SECRETS OF ENOCH'S WALK WITH GOD

The New Testament emphasizes that the same standard of judgment you apply to others will be used to judge you (Matthew 7:2). What it doesn't reveal is how quickly that judgment may return—like a boomerang.

Scripture consistently teaches that the most vital interpersonal ethic is self-examination, not condemnation or scorn toward others. Psalm 1 teaches us. Yet, this foundational principle is rarely echoed from today's pulpits. Instead, many have been divided and intoxicated by teachings rooted in sensuality, racial bias, and flesh-centered ideologies. These views often come from those who consider themselves "well-informed" and "spirit-led," yet they use their perceived insight to judge not just ideas—but people.

Yet the true practice of the faith of God is in this:

> Examine yourselves to see whether you are in the faith; test yourselves. Do you not realize that Christ Jesus is in you —unless, of course, you fail the test? And I trust that you will discover that we have not failed the test.
>
> ∞ 2 Corinthians 13:5-6 NIV ∞

The examination one needs to pass is not the one given you by another person but the exam of faith God assesses you by. A careful unhindered examination of oneself, unless you are cheating yourself, is one of the best ways in which we open to God.

Unless we know our own brokenness and where we need the Potter to put us back together, how can we know what kind of best person we should be? Let alone dream about becoming the vessel of honor set aside for the Master's use? Any human being regardless of their estate can fool the other person next to them. But if one engages in fooling themselves what hope is there for such a person before God who weighs the hearts?

> Your heart will meditate on terror: "Where is the scribe? Where is he who weighs? Where is he who counts the towers?"
>
> ∞ Isaiah 33:18 NKJV ∞

Beyond a focus on the present troubles, environment, and the pursuit of gratifying oneself, just a good meditation away, lies a sure and lasting foundation. Look past your fears of what is around you and boldly diminish the terror and its perpetrators.

The enigma of power lies in the fact that what you fear and strive to appease can imprison you. Conversely, what you resist and downplay by ignoring loses its influence. So, in this, you see the dimension of Enoch's testimony not being one of fear or dread of God but one of pleasing and reverence.

It would not make sense before God and neither before us if God commanded fear in the context of terror toward His creation. Reverence, decency, and respect are not weak character traits. They are in fact the bedrock of a sweet relationship. This is what Enoch had towards God and His host. This man was so in tune with the heavenly order of decorum that he accessed realms of the heavens and wisdom that most of us still struggle to wrap our understanding around.

THE SECRETS OF ENOCH'S WALK WITH GOD

Seven Keys to Understanding Enoch's Walk with God

Meditate on these truths drawn from his extraordinary life.

1. Fearless Devotion to God Alone

- Enoch did not fear angels, demons, principalities, or any spiritual entity.
- Unlike many modern believers who fear witch doctors, political figures, or hidden agendas, Enoch's reverence was reserved for God alone.
- The greatest error is to ascribe fear to anything or anyone other than God.

For deeper reflection, see Chapter 25: Be Careful Of Meditation On Fear.

2. Unwavering Personal Faith

- Enoch's faith was not outsourced to a church, prophet, or intercessor—it was personal and steadfast.
- He trusted God's plans and walked in agreement with Him.
- Faith is the foundation of pleasing God, and it must be rooted in personal trust, obedience, and reliance.

"Can two walk together unless they are agreed?" (Amos 3:3)

3. Radical Obedience to God

- Enoch's life was marked by complete obedience to God's commands.
- His walk was so pleasing to God that he transitioned from time into eternity—one of only three known to ascend without tasting death (Enoch, Elijah, and Jesus).

4. Intimate Communion and Worship

- Enoch was a wise leader and counselor, yet he was called apart for deep fellowship with God.
- He spent significant time in the presence of God and His angels, engaging in prayer, meditation, and worship.
- God spoke to Enoch from His throne, revealing mysteries of creation, cosmic balance, and the forces of nature.

5. Upright Living and Intercession

- Enoch lived with a constant awareness of God's presence—a trait of seasoned meditation.
- When the watcher angels fell and took human wives, Enoch interceded, delivering their petition to God and conveying His response.

THE SECRETS OF ENOCH'S WALK WITH GOD

6. Prophetic Insight and Revelation

- Enoch is considered the first prophet after Adam's fall.
- He had deep insight into God's plans, judgments, and heavenly order.
- His prophetic role made him a sought-after leader until God instructed him to hide himself.
- He understood the end times and possessed profound scientific and spiritual knowledge.

Paul exhorts us to seek the gift of prophecy (1 Corinthians 14:1).

7. Clear Identity and Spiritual Discipline

- Enoch knew who he was—not just morally, but spiritually.
- True discipline flows from knowing your divine identity and authority.
- Like the centurion who understood authority, Enoch walked in clarity and purpose, unhindered by confusion about his role.

Chapter 25

BE CAREFUL OF MEDITATION ON FEAR

> Your mind will meditate on the terror: [asking] Where is he who counted? Where is he who weighed the tribute? Where is he who counted the towers?
>
> ∞ Isaiah 33:18 AMPC ∞

The context of the scripture above is quite simple. It speaks of destroyers, betrayers, treaty breakers, and despisers within and around Israel as a nation who were caught up in the prophetic message. The prophet Isaiah begins to point out by the Spirit of the LORD that when God delivers us, we can look back and meditate on the terror that has passed and we will not see these arrogant plunderers counting their loot.

When reading the full chapter where this verse is interned, you can realize there are safeguards against falling prey to the machinations of the wicked ones. The biggest bluff Satan can have on any of us is to make us fearful of his agents, their rhetoric, their acts of plunder. What tends to happen with any person faced with terror is we tend to be reactive and passive defensive. We see the problem, react in fear to it and our first line of defense is to pull away.

This is a general mode of seeking equilibrium of the status quo. There is a difference between seeking peace with a sister or brother that you do not agree with and finding peace between you and an enemy who has no regard for your estate. To a sister or brother, you can give ground and room for accommodation but to the one plundering your harvest or taking your vineyards, you erect a resistance wall against his excursions as a way of finding balance while seeking to establish a balanced line of communication.

There is always a weapon or weakness used to instill fear. The biggest weakness any of us have is our life or that of our loved ones as we perceive it. The normalcy of this life is what is always targeted by our enemies as our weakness.

The way this 33rd chapter of Isaiah talks about the meditation on fear is by pointing us to be in a position where our fear is one, we hold in high esteem to give it only to God as a reverential fear. I could pick on many scriptures to show you that the LORD (Adonai) is the only one to whom fear should be ascribed. Neither should I seek for anyone around me to fear me. The God in us, the Creator of all is the one to hold in reverential fear, honoring Him.

> The LORD is exalted, for He dwells on high; He will fill Zion with His justice and righteousness. He will be the sure foundation for your times, a rich store of salvation and wisdom and knowledge; the fear of the LORD is the key to this treasure.
>
> ∞ Isaiah 33:5-6 BSB ∞

Jesus taught us that we should not be afraid of people.

> Then Jesus said to the people, "I tell you, my friends, don't be afraid of people. They can kill the body, but after that they can do nothing more to hurt you. I will show you the one to fear. You should fear God, who has the power to kill you and also to throw you into hell. Yes, he is the one you should fear.
>
> ∞ Luke 12:4-6 ERV ∞

BE CAREFUL OF MEDITATION ON FEAR

It is clear as crystal that we are admonished to fear God, not men nor angels nor anything that God created, or men has conjured up. There were men and women of God with no weapon but just a mindset resident on God. They looked at a calamity and calmed it down making it put its tail between its legs like a harmless bulldog. History is full of these.

There was resistance to occupation, colonization, racism, or marginalization that overcame the scourge of these deplorable tendencies with just a steady voice of resistance.

Problems arising from fear are encumbered upon us more when we doubt our voice, who we are, and what the God we serve can accomplish through us. The law of nature is clear one cannot walk on the surface of deep liquid water unless they are using a flotation device.

Even with a flotation device, one cannot perfectly balance one's standing and movement on the surface of water. The deck of the natural laws of gravity, buoyancy, and water surface tension stacks heavily in favor of drowning whoever attempts to walk on water. Reasonable calculations make fear an acceptable judgment and understanding.

The voice of reason is always grounded in fact. However, when it comes to fear and overcoming the voice of reason that favors fear, remember Jesus. Don't be afraid of people. Don't be afraid of death, evil, witches, sickness, powers or principalities, and dominions.

If fear rears its head up, know it is a messenger of a sinister wave of deception riding the fear to make you do nothing or succumb to its rider. When Jesus bids you come to Him walking on water. Observe Him and how He does it and care not to observe the water, its physical properties, and your physical characteristics as pertain to the water, unless you plan to go to Him swimming in it.

Notice, that Jesus did not say fear is evil. What makes it bad for you is to whom you hold it. The one who projects fear into you may not be bad, evil, or intent on doing you bad. The aspect of holding yourself in fear, even of parents, children, siblings, or friends becomes a limitation to you.

Fear hinders your full obedience to God. Fear can influence your decisions, and it can cause you to sideline the voice of the Holy Spirit. Fear, bias, and prejudice work hand in hand if one does not check them. Where these are exhibits in people towards others, they easily persecute those who are "different" from them.

After reading this chapter, pause. Have a "higgaion" moment. Meditate on ways to recover your ground and stand where your fear is only for God going forward.

Chapter 26

WHATSOEVER VIRTUOUS THINGS MEDITATION

> Finally, brethren, whatsoever things are true, whatsoever things are honest, whatsoever things are just, whatsoever things are pure, whatsoever things are lovely, whatsoever things are of good report; if there be any virtue, and if there be any praise, think on these things. Those things, which ye have both learned, and received, and heard, and seen in me, do: and the God of peace shall be with you.
>
> ∞ Philippians 4:8-9 KJV ∞

This is one of the best prescription scriptures in the Bible. It makes it easier to know what to keep your mind focused on, what to meditate on, and how you can discover what you are best at doing.

The phrase *"think on these things"* would seem contrary to when Jesus taught, *"take no thought of"* certain things. If you look deeper, the Philippians verse is not asking you to worry over the *'whatsoever things'*. Jesus on the other hand taught us not to worry over our daily provisions because God already knows we need them and have already been provided.

But *'whatsoever things'* are virtues that build character and are not meat and drink per se. Whatsoever things are the very building blocks that help us find our calling, our voice, and our identity.

'Whatsoever things' is such a huge classification for *things true, honest, just, pure, lovely, of good report, virtuous, and praiseworthy*. Regardless of our challenges and problems, we have some things we can tune our thinking (meditation) frequencies to and rise and do more of them.

Have you ever paused to meditate on whatever is good, noble, and pure? This is one of the most powerful ways to guard your heart and mind from becoming a workshop for the enemy.

MEDITATING THROUGH THE BIBLE

While the woman with the alabaster box was immersed in a Holy Spirit-inspired act of worship—anointing Jesus' feet with costly perfume—Judas Iscariot was busy plotting betrayal. His heart had long ceased to dwell on things that are good and godly. He scorned the woman's prophetic act, not because of its spiritual significance, but because he couldn't profit from the perfume's value.

Judas went on to offer Jesus to the Sanhedrin Council, perhaps justifying his actions by imagining that such a move would spark a rebellion against both the Council and Rome for persecuting Jesus. But his motives were far from pure.

The woman once marked by shame highly valued the feet of Jesus—what He stood for and the unmatched worth His presence brought—far more than the alabaster oil. This time, she was free, no longer using such a precious fragrance to indulge men who once marked her for their comfort.

Paul goes on to admonish about *'those things'* he exemplified by teaching, giving, listening to, and doing that are part of the whatsoever things. These things Paul exhorted the disciples of Jesus to emulate. Paul did not second-guess his faith, work, and example. He was a sure witness. Paul was confident and unwavering in his beliefs, his efforts, and the way he lived his life.

The best way to be fulfilled in life is not to be sorely consumed by filling the stomach or the house with dainties. The great apostle came to understand that meditating on virtuous and godly thoughts brings a peace that surpasses all understanding.

We find fulfillment when we do good to others. This is why the vilest and angriest souls often remain restless, even with full stomachs and lavish possessions. King Saul, Jezebel, King Ahab, and Pharaoh all died in disgrace, having been used by the sin that crouched at their door to persecute those whom God had blessed.

WHATSOEVER VIRTUOUS THINGS MEDITATION

Likewise, the one who is stingy—who hoards abundance and refuses to share with the needy—cannot truly be at peace. Generosity and virtue are the pathways to lasting fulfillment.

Be on the lookout for whatsoever things. They tend to go unnoticed by those who get stuck *BUSY (being under Satan's yoke)* and lose being *steadfastly meditating articulating real transformation (SMART)*.

For those who dream and see visions that are transformative by nature, meditation on 'whatsoever things' is a source of inspiration and answers more than it is a problem.

Do you have some 'whatsoever things' you think about daily? Do you dream? Do you see visions? Do you meditate?

Desire to truly see the "whatsoever things" spoken of in Scripture and exercise yourself in them.

Seeing, in this context, often goes beyond physical sight. It refers to the inner vision—mental images, understanding, wisdom, and spiritual insight. To "see" is to visualize, to dream, to perceive with the heart and mind.

When we fail to see in this way, we miss out on the experience of divine revelation and purpose. That kind of blindness makes the manifestation of good things a rare phenomenon. Yet, we are all capable of seeing and bringing these good and virtuous things into reality.

The difference lies in choice. Some choose to walk in light and truth, while others willingly become sons and daughters of Belial—rejecting what is good and embracing what is vile.

Chapter 27

THE LORD'S PRAYER AND YOUR NEEDS

> Then, turning to his disciples, Jesus said, "That is why I tell you not to worry about everyday life—whether you have enough food to eat or enough clothes to wear. For life is more than food, and your body more than clothing.
>
> ∞ Luke 12:22-23 NLT ∞

I recommend meditatively studying the LORD's Prayer together with Luke Chapter 12.

Luke 12 is a rich chapter filled with Jesus' teachings on trust, priorities, and spiritual vigilance. One of its central themes is freedom from anxiety—especially concerning material needs like food and clothing. Jesus teaches that worrying over daily provisions is not only unnecessary but spiritually misaligned. He reminds His followers that life is more than food and the body more than clothing (Luke 12:22–31). Instead of dwelling on lack, Jesus calls us to trust in God's faithful provision.

This teaching stands in contrast to how many approach prayer today—often coming before God with deep anxiety over material concerns. Jesus redirects our focus from worry-driven meditation (dwelling mentally on fear or scarcity) to faith-driven trust. This shift is essential to understanding the heart of prayer as Jesus taught it.

In Matthew 6, Jesus critiques the empty, repetitive prayers of religious leaders and pagans—prayers that were long, loud, and performance-based. He warns against babbling and showiness, emphasizing that God is not impressed by many words but by sincere hearts. Jesus then offers the Lord's Prayer as a model—not just for what to say, but how to pray:

MEDITATING THROUGH THE BIBLE

- **Worship:** *"Our Father in heaven, hallowed be Your name."*
- **Submission:** *"Your kingdom come, Your will be done."*
- **Petition:** *"Give us this day our daily bread."*
- **Repentance and forgiveness:** *"Forgive us our debts…"*
- **Spiritual protection:** *"Deliver us from evil."*

Notice how "Give us our daily bread" is a brief, trusting request—not a long, anxious plea. This aligns perfectly with Luke 12's message: don't meditate on lack; trust God's care.

Jesus is not discouraging prayer—He's refining it. He teaches us to replace anxious meditation with peaceful trust, and to pray with clarity, humility, and faith. His instructions can be summarized as:

- **Don't worry – pray:** *Prayers rooted in anxiety are ineffective.*
- **Don't babble:** *Long, showy prayers don't impress God.*
- **Do trust:** *Meditate on God's goodness and provision.*
- **Do pray simply:** *Ask with faith, not fear.*

Here's a helpful comparison:

Meditation	Prayer
Internal reflection, often prolonged & silent	Direct communication with God
Make it positive (on God's Word) not negative (worry, needy)	Should be sincere, focused, and brief
Jesus warns against meditating on fear and worry, Luke 12	Jesus teaches to ask simply and trustingly-Matthew 6
Can shape your mindset and emotions	Invites divine intervention and relationship
Typically, silent or guided with minimal verbal input	Often verbal or mental (spoken, sung, or silent)

THE LORD'S PRAYER AND YOUR NEEDS

Jesus' teachings in Luke 12 and Matthew 6 are deeply connected. He calls us to a life of trust, not fear. He's not discouraging prayer—He's refining it. He's teaching us to replace anxious meditation with peaceful trust, and to pray. He invites us to pray—not with anxiety or performance—but with faith, clarity, simplicity, humility, and confidence in God's care.

> And when you pray, do not babble on like pagans, for they think that by their many words, they will be heard. Do not be like them, for your Father knows what you need before you ask Him.
>
> So then, this is how you should pray:
>
> 'Our Father in heaven, hallowed be Your name. Your kingdom come, Your will be done, on earth as it is in heaven. Give us this day our daily bread. And forgive us our debts, as we also have forgiven our debtors.
>
> And lead us not into temptation, but deliver us from the evil one.'
>
> ∞ Matthew 6:7-13 BSB ∞

Many worshippers today tend to focus more on presenting their needs—such as requests for food, clothing, and other necessities—than on offering heartfelt praise, worship, and meditation to God. As a result, prayer often becomes a series of petitions rather than a profound encounter with the divine, lacking the personal revelation of who God truly is to the one praying.

MEDITATING THROUGH THE BIBLE

> And it shall come to pass, that before they call, I will answer; and while they are yet speaking, I will hear.
>
> ∞ Isaiah 65:24 KJV ∞

Too often, people pray with intense urgency and frequency only when they are in need. This pattern can make it seem as though God is being treated like an errand servant—called upon solely to fulfill requests. The contrast becomes clear when that same fervor is absent during times of abundance.

This mindset stems from a common misunderstanding: we forget that God is already aware of our needs before we even speak them. As Scripture says, 'Before you call, I will answer.' This suggests that God begins responding the moment we start to meditate on our needs.

In the stillness of meditation, we can discern God's heart and align ourselves with His provision. When we truly trust that our needs are already met, our prayers shift from anxious pleading to peaceful communion. We no longer approach God with worry, but with faith and gratitude.

If God already knows what we need, then repeatedly begging as though He is unwilling to provide may unintentionally portray Him as stingy or distant. Instead, we are called to rest in His goodness, confident that He is both aware of our needs and faithful to meet them.

> And seek not ye what ye shall eat, and what ye shall drink, neither be ye of doubtful mind. For all these things do the nations of the world seek after: but your Father knoweth that ye have need of these things. Yet seek ye his kingdom, and these things shall be added unto you.
>
> ∞ Luke 12:29-31 ASV ∞

THE LORD'S PRAYER AND YOUR NEEDS

The keys to effective prayers given in the scriptures above are:

1. Meditate Before You Ask

   a. Don't rush to present your needs in prayer. Instead, take time to meditate on what God has already provided. In that stillness, you'll often find that the answer is already unfolding.

2. Trust in God's Provision

   a. If you truly believe that God knows your needs, then trust that He has already made provision for them. Doubting His ability only hinders your faith.

3. Prioritize God's Kingdom

   a. Seek first the Kingdom of God—not just what you need. When your heart is aligned with His purposes, everything else falls into place.

4. Recognize the Inheritance

   a. God's Kingdom is not distant or inaccessible; it's available for you to possess. Step into it with confidence and faith.

5. Your Needs Are Already Included

   a. The blessings of God's Kingdom come with everything you need. Your provisions are not separate—they're part of the package that comes with walking in His will.

> And you, do not seek [by meditating and reasoning to inquire into] what you are to eat and what you are to drink; nor be of anxious (troubled) mind [unsettled, excited, worried, and in suspense];
>
> ∞ Luke 12:29 AMPC ∞

MEDITATING THROUGH THE BIBLE

Prayer is solemn. So is meditating on God's Word to hear from Him. I trust this chapter will open new ways in which you begin to meditate and pray differently.

Here is my understanding of what Jesus taught and how we ought to pray.

Meditation Is the Key Preface to Prayer

This is by far the most forgotten aspect concerning prayer. Before prayer, meditate. Know why and how you are praying. Does anyone who has no clue and will not observe the etiquette associated with the authority approach an earthly king or even a judge and not be admonished first? Do not disqualify yourself by ignorance regarding how you ought to pray. Remember, the one who truly (follows protocol) comes before God, He never ignores them (John 6:37)

Joshua's commission emphasized meditation as the primary key to good success. As Moses' minister, Joshua was already dedicated to staying, praying, and worshipping at the Tabernacle. But for the next level, God's guidance highlighted the importance of meditating on His precepts. This principle applies to us as well.

It is essential that one self-weed out hypocritical and selfish tendencies in oneself before one comes before Him. No one is immune to this. To the veterans, who have walked with God for a long while, and the ones approaching Him today, God holds the same respect.

There is no preferential treatment with God. Veteran worshippers should be wary of complacency and pride stemming from their past and present experiences.

THE LORD'S PRAYER AND YOUR NEEDS

Know Who God Is to You

The most common mistake we make as believers is to not take God as our Father. This should be our first instinct and inclination. If we do not do so, we become subjects or servants, not heirs of His promises and His inheritance. "Our Father, who art in heaven" personalizes our relationship with God.

Know Your Identity

This easily follows from the preceding point. Sons and daughters of an earthly king approach the king and the throne differently.

Subjects approach the throne whereas heirs approach the unlimited grace of a father. Subjects are bound by protocol to the throne while sons and daughters are bound to the heart of the king as children.

If picturing a throne room, sons and daughters occupy the front row and may come up to the king's seat.

> Oh that I knew where I might find him! That I might come even to his seat!
>
> ∞ Job 23:3 KJV ∞

Subjects of the throne bow standing below and away from the king's seat.

Take your pick where you want to stand. This is what knowing your identity entails. So, when in prayer or in meditation, if you so much doubt your worth, you cannot receive anything. To both the servant and the child, we come boldly before the throne.

> Let us therefore come boldly unto the throne of grace, that we may obtain mercy, and find grace to help in time of need.
>
> ∞ Hebrews 4:16 KJV ∞

Extol Him

Jesus teaching us to pray, makes it plain that we should extol God. Remember worrisome prayers are not the way of approach no matter how much distress you are in. "All is well" was the confession of the Shunammite woman. "Hallowed be Your name" means you and I actively keep God's name holy, revered throughout life.

> Run at once to meet her and say to her, 'Is all well with you? Is all well with your husband? Is all well with the child?'" And she answered, "All is well."
>
> ∞ 2 Kings 4:26 ESV ∞

This Shunammite woman was not denied anything before an earthly king. Even the prophet to whom God did not disclose why she approached the prophet outside of the appointed time was compelled to entreat God differently for her sake. Her favor was so great, that I seek to connect every time to the grace God afforded her.

THE LORD'S PRAYER AND YOUR NEEDS

> And when the king asked the woman, she told him. So the king appointed unto her a certain officer, saying, Restore all that was hers, and all the fruits of the field since the day that she left the land, even until now.
>
> ∞ 2 Kings 8:6 ESV ∞

Accept God's Kingdom and Will in Your Flesh

Most people desire to see the kingdom of God and His will being done on the greater earth. There is no doubt about this.

Yet most do not want to accept His kingdom and His will in their flesh or earth. This is the biggest obstacle. It does not work that way. God did not fulfill his desire for the earth by creating it but by putting a man in fellowship with Him in the garden to tend and keep it.

His kingdom and his will must first reign over our flesh and the earth will align. If it is the other way round, there will not be found any place upon the earth for those whose hearts are not aligned to Him.

What phrases of the LORD's prayer speak of His Kingdom and will?

Place a Demand for Today's Bread

The phrase "give us" is an imperative form, understood as a request or command. Even in the original writings, it stands out as a demand. Now bear in mind that even subjects of a kingdom can place a demand on the crown.

MEDITATING THROUGH THE BIBLE

To petition or pray for the kingdom people's needs, as if the crown does not intend to give it to them, will insult the throne. Know this from numerous scriptures: even before we ask, God has already made provision.

> Death and life are in the power of the tongue, and they who indulge in it shall eat the fruit of it [for death or life].
>
> ∞ Proverbs 18:21 AMPC ∞

The biggest reason why people end up not seeing their needs manifested, even after praying, is what we confess in the prayer. Let's assume your meditation before prayer is acceptable, the protocol is observed. What defiles a man? The words that come from our mouths. Death and life, are they not in the power of the tongue?

The key is what you confess after prayers. Humans can decipher when someone you know does not mean what they say. How much more God? Who has uttered words to God that are void of faith and intent and received a positive answer?

Does the prodigal son's teaching not show that, if we are His children, He gives us what we ask even when we don't deserve it? Did the prodigal son not have faith that the father would give him what he asked?

Where the prodigal son was tested and found lacking faith was in understanding that his error (sin) did not disqualify him as a son nor was his provision tied to his sin. God sends rain, seed time, and harvest on both the evil and the just alike.

But our provision can be astonishingly fabulous if we can be kingdom minded.

THE LORD'S PRAYER AND YOUR NEEDS

Accept Forgiveness to the Extent You Give It to Others

Here is a mystery and a truth. The LORD's prayer does not explicitly mention healing. But forgiveness and bread were mentioned in how mankind should handle them and how God receives us.

There seems to be a conditional aspect to God's forgiveness implied in Jesus' statement, "And forgive us our debts, as we also have forgiven our debtors". It suggests that our forgiveness from God is linked to our willingness to forgive others. This idea is echoed in other parts of the Bible, such as in Matthew 6:14-15, where it states that if we forgive others, God will forgive us, but if we do not forgive others, God will not forgive us.

I can never over-emphasize why forgiveness is important for one's healing. It is true that by covering forgiveness, Jesus covered healing in the LORD's prayer. Prominent teachers of the Bible who prayed for the sick in their meetings made it a point to stress the significance of forgiveness to their audience members before praying for them. The following Bible verse says it all. Confession of sin should be followed by forgiveness.

> So confess your sins to one another and pray for one another so that you may be healed. The prayer of a righteous person has great effectiveness.
>
> ∞ James 5:16 NET ∞

When looking at the Lord's prayer and considering modern-day medical, nutritional, and psychological studies it is a fact that food, forgiveness, and meditation are like medicine to the human body and psych.

Ever wondered why? The ones who eat healthily and forgive those who trespass against them live healthy, longer, and fulfilled lives.

MEDITATING THROUGH THE BIBLE

Led by the Spirit away from Evil

The significance of Jesus teaching us to pray that we don't fall into temptation is huge. The Spirit of God led Jesus after His baptism into the wilderness where He fasted 40 days. At the end of the fast, the story of the tempter coming to Him with options resonant with our daily lives.

The difference between Jesus's story and most of ours is that we let our lusts (of the eyes, the flesh, and the pride of life) lead us and not the Spirit of God. If we are led by the Spirit, we will win and overcome. However, if we are led by our greed, the best outcome we can hope for is to come out of any situation with all our limbs intact.

To be led by the Spirit guarantees we are always safe from the evil. Just as Jesus overcame, so do we. What was Jesus' meditation while fasting in the wilderness like? What was revealed to Him to the extent no amount of *gifts* Satan offered could sway Him.

Now consider if this was an offer Satan made to someone led by anything other than the Spirit of God. What could have been the outcome? Jesus had impeccable discernment to know the devil's intentions hidden behind a seemingly *"fine suggestion"* for a hungry Jesus to turn stones into bread and eat. Jesus did not live by bread alone.

Do you live by bread alone? Have a discerning mind and spirit. Not all "fine suggestions" are good. Eve was caught in the hidden net of such a suggestion.

Who and What Is This Prayer For?

The conclusion of the Lord's Prayer reveals both the intended audience and the purpose of the kind of prayer Jesus taught. Remember His words: "Seek

THE LORD'S PRAYER AND YOUR NEEDS

first the Kingdom." This raises a vital question—for whom and for what is your prayer truly intended?

The answer to that question holds the key to receiving "all these things" that are promised to be "added unto you." The ability to receive what you need is directly tied to your commitment to advancing God's Kingdom, not just your personal desires.

Take time to return to the drawing board. Meditate deeply on how you are seeking God's Kingdom.

Chapter 28

IS THE BUSH BURNING?
-A MEDITATION

> Resolve and settle it in your mind not to meditate and prepare beforehand how you are to make your defense and how you will answer.
>
> ∞ Luke 21:14 AMPC ∞

There are two instances where meditation is not a required pre-requisite according to Jesus:

1. The first is about what you shall eat, drink, or wear.

2. The second is concerning persecutions enforced through prosecutorial means.

> Now when they take you [to court] and put you under arrest, do not be anxious beforehand about what you are to say nor [even] meditate about it; but say whatever is given you in that hour and at the moment, for it is not you who will be speaking, but the Holy Spirit.
>
> ∞ Mark 13:11 AMPC ∞

At first glance, Jesus' teaching about not preparing a defense when facing persecution might seem outdated—especially in the context of modern legal systems. Today, anyone accused in a court of law is entitled to legal representation, and having a competent attorney is considered essential. While lacking such representation is uncommon, it's not unheard of.

However, Jesus wasn't speaking about ordinary legal disputes or civil infractions. He was addressing persecution rooted in faith—opposition faced because of one's allegiance to Him, association with fellow believers, or commitment to moral conviction. This isn't about defending oneself against wrongdoing; it's about standing firm when righteousness itself is on trial. The moral and godly precepts, though not codified in a society's laws fall in this category if persecution arises for standing by them.

In such moments, Jesus promises divine assistance: "Do not worry about what to say or how to say it. At that time you will be given what to say." This is a call to yield to the Holy Spirit, trusting that He will speak through you when your faith is challenged.

Does this sound familiar? Think of Moses before Pharaoh, declaring with boldness, "Thus says the Lord God of Israel: Let my people go!" Moses didn't rely on persuasive arguments or legal counsel—he relied on the authority and voice of God.

In the same way, Jesus invites us to trust that when we stand for Him, we won't stand alone. The Spirit will give us the words, the wisdom, and the courage we need.

This brings me to share my insights on one of the most iconic God encounters of all time: the burning bush - Moses' encounter with God. I am approaching this from a meditative point of view.

The story of the burning bush, as described in the Book of Exodus, is one of the most profound and symbolic narratives in the Bible. Was this encounter on an ordinary path Moses had passed through in the 40 years he had been in Midian? Was there a bush that had always burned in this spot? Had anyone else seen it? Is this a portal of immense connection with heaven that is still available today?

IS THE BUSH BURNING? A MEDITATION

Moses miraculously encounters God, through a bush that burns but is not consumed. It would be a gross mistake to take this event as just a historical or religious anecdote. It carries deep spiritual significance that can be applied to our lives today. The burning bush represents a divine encounter, a call to purpose, and a turning point from a runaway failed prince to an enigmatic deliverer and a human god feat.

Firstly, let us carefully look at the thoughts (meditation) of Moses when he encounters the burning bush.

> And Moses said, I will now turn aside and see this great sight, why the bush is not burned. And when the Lord saw that he turned aside to see, God called to him out of the midst of the bush and said, Moses, Moses! And he said, Here am I.
>
> ∞ Exodus 3:3-4 AMP ∞

Moses saw the bush burning without any consumption of its estate. He did not ignore or disregard the appearance of a phenomenon or wonder before him. He turned aside to see *(perceive with the eyes; discern visually; take it in; discern or deduce mentally after reflection or meditation; and understand)* why the bush was not consumed into ashes.

Notice that when Moses turned aside to look at the burning bush, God spoke to him from within it. His turning wasn't a casual glance—it was a deliberate act of attention and consideration. It made God speak to him. This is where many people miss their divine encounters: they don't turn aside. They remain preoccupied with the noise of life, failing to pause and reflect on the seemingly insignificant moments that may carry eternal significance.

The bush itself was ordinary, but the fire burning within it was not. The miracle wasn't in the bush—it was in the presence and voice of God revealed through it. The lesson? Pay attention to the fire's voice, not just the spectacle.

For this meditation, let's not dwell on the conversation Moses had with God, but rather explore his attitude before, during, and after the encounter. This is crucial for believers today. It's not that we lack encounters with God—it's that we often fail to engage them deeply enough to receive insight, transformation, and empowerment.

Moses wasn't praying when the encounter happened. He was seeking to understand, which is a meditative posture. He had led his father-in-law's sheep to the far side of the desert. At eighty years old, he wasn't tending his own flock, and his status was far from glorious—especially when compared to Jacob. Yet in that moment, Moses chose to pursue the mystery before him rather than remain focused on the sheep. The sheep probably behaved better during his encounter.

So, ask yourself: What matters more to you today? Is it Pharaoh's demands? The taskmasters' expectations? The sheep of your obligations? Or the sign God keeps placing before you to catch your attention?

When God called Moses by name, Moses recognized the voice and responded. He made himself present in God's presence—not by words, but by obedience. He followed God's instruction and stopped approaching the bush. This is significant: God often uses signs to draw our attention, but once He has it, the focus must shift from the sign to His voice.

The wind, the storm, the lightning, the thunder, and the fire are not meant to be followed—they are meant to lead us to the voice. Have you missed the mark by following the sign, when you should have followed the voice within the sign?

IS THE BUSH BURNING? A MEDITATION

> For the Jews require a sign, and the Greeks seek after wisdom:
>
> ∞ 1 Corinthians 1:22 KJV ∞

In Jesus' time, Jews sought signs and Greeks pursued wisdom. Yet when the One who embodied both appeared, they stumbled—offended by His words, blind to His wonders. The Greeks recoiled at the idea of consuming His flesh; the Sanhedrin condemned Him for claiming equality with God. Don't miss the voice behind the signs. Look beyond the wonders to perceive the truth.

Moses took off his shoes. In that moment, the man who would be called the most humble (Numbers 12:3) began to be reshaped. Once a prince of Egypt, a murderer, a rejected deliverer, and a poor son-in-law with no army against a mighty king—he removed the shoes that carried the weight of his past identity and authority.

Shoes symbolize our journey, our history, the ground we claim, and the lens through which we interpret life. By removing them, Moses surrendered his story to God, stepping into a new identity shaped not by status or failure, but by divine purpose.

Moses covered his face in reverence to God.

Why is this significant? The face represents identity—our image, our uniqueness, much like a fingerprint. When Moses turned to see the burning bush, he was drawn by wonder. But when he heard God's voice, he covered his face—not the bush, not the voice.

This act wasn't about shielding himself from God but about humbling his own identity before the One speaking. It was a moment of surrender, not self-display. Moses didn't come to showcase who he was; he came to listen, to yield, to be transformed.

MEDITATING THROUGH THE BIBLE

Reverence to God begins when we stop projecting ourselves and start honoring the One who calls us.

Here lies the biggest mistake most make. A God encounter where you do not lay aside your identity, being and self-projection cannot change you for the better. God works with what you surrender to Him and not what you cannot give Him.

Moses learned to shed his identity and take on God's by recognizing what he could surrender. He never made himself the face of the mission. Though he left the burning bush in Midian, he carried God's voice from it with him. The fire that consumed the bush didn't stay behind—it took residence in Moses. Moses became the burning bush, a living flame, a light to lead.

When Moses tried to retreat into his stammering identity and limitations, God had already moved beyond them.

God wasn't focused on Moses' weaknesses—He was commissioning him as a god to Pharaoh, with Aaron as his prophet. From the burning bush onward, Moses was transformed. That encounter didn't just mark a moment; it shaped a man. The rest of his journey reveals how deeply Moses was changed by the voice he heard and the fire he carried.

Imagine from a distance seeing Moses covering his face, falling to the ground before a bush, and speaking to the bush. A natural mind cannot see the fire in the bush, and neither can it hear the voice of God from the burning bush. If this was a familiar or unfamiliar path to Moses, we would not know.

The hint we get is that this was the "backside", meaning not usually chartered. Most God encounters are through unchartered manifestations. You could look at Enoch, Noah, Abraham, Sarah, Hagar, Isaac, Jacob, Rebekah Samuel, Ruth, Gideon, King David, Solomon, Elijah, Elisha, Daniel, Hosea, and John the Baptist. None of their encounters were the same.

IS THE BUSH BURNING? A MEDITATION

But God's voice remains the same. It is the creative force that transforms and creates everything. This is also why your individual voice matters. We all don't have to be deliverers. We become His voice when we receive God's word and visitation through whom He sends to minister to us.

God's word gets transformed into what it accomplishes not returning void back to Him. It returns as a people free to speak their voice, freedom, knowledge, and wisdom. This is the liberty of faith and receiving God's word.

> A truly wise person uses few words; a person with understanding is even-tempered.
>
> ∞ Proverbs 17:27 NLT ∞

How does a human voice become God's voice?

It happens when a person speaks what God is saying—not when they speak from their own will and expect divine endorsement. The authority of God's voice flows through a life surrendered to His Spirit.

When the Spirit of the Lord dwells within, He informs and leads our wisdom, understanding, counsel, power, and reverence. That divine presence is the difference-maker—taking over and transforming the human voice into a vocal frequency of God's truth and transformative power.

MEDITATING THROUGH THE BIBLE

> And the spirit of the LORD shall rest upon him, the spirit of wisdom and understanding, the spirit of counsel and might, the spirit of knowledge and of the fear of the LORD;
>
> ∞ Isaiah 11:2 ESV ∞

Is the Bush Burning?

This question invites deep reflection: Have you truly encountered God?

Has His presence transformed you—inside and out?

Moses' encounter at the burning bush was not a fleeting moment. Though he left the bush behind, the voice and fire of God never left him. He became the burning bush—carrying the flame, speaking with divine authority, and shining with purpose.

A true God encounter doesn't just inspire—it inhabits. It turns us into vessels of grace, healing, and light. We become living flames that do not burn out, through which God speaks and moves.

To be the burning bush is to embrace your divine calling. It's a reminder that your life has meaning, shaped by purpose and guided by God. Whether through your work, relationships, service, or passions, the fire within you is meant to shine.

Fire purifies, empowers, and reveals God's presence. The burning bush symbolizes a faith that endures—alive, vibrant, and unshaken by trials. When we carry that fire, we walk with hope, resilience, and clarity, even in the darkest times.

IS THE BUSH BURNING? A MEDITATION

Moses was transformed—and so can we be. Let us turn aside, listen deeply, and become the habitation of God. Let our lives burn with purpose, not consumed, but continually refined by divine encounter.

> You have said, Seek My face [inquire for and require My presence as your vital need]. My heart says to You, Your face (Your presence), Lord, will I seek, inquire for, and require [of necessity and on the authority of Your Word]
>
> ∞ Psalm 27:8 AMPC ∞

Are You a Burning Bush? Does your encounter with God inspire and guide you? Can you confidently say He is with you, leading you, and calling you to a divine mission? Are you a burning bush- lit and alive with His voice, radiating His presence?

Be discerning. Stay connected to the source of life and purpose. Let your relationship with God shape your wisdom, decisions, and direction. A true encounter with Him doesn't just transform you—it empowers you to transform others.

Moses' burning bush moment wasn't just about his personal calling; it was the beginning of a nation's liberation. When God's fire burns within us, it reminds us that our purpose reaches beyond ourselves. We're called to be light-bearers, healers, and builders in our communities.

Fire, across spiritual traditions, symbolizes purification, passion, and divine presence. The burning bush is a picture of enduring faith—alive, resilient, and unconsumed by trials. When we carry that flame, we become vessels of hope, illuminating paths even in the darkest seasons.

MEDITATING THROUGH THE BIBLE

Let your encounter with God make you a living flame—His voice through your life, His purpose in your steps, His presence in your being.

> And suddenly the LORD said to Moses, Aaron, and Miriam, "You three, come out to the Tent of Meeting." So the three went out, and the LORD came down in a pillar of cloud, stood at the entrance to the Tent, and summoned Aaron and Miriam.
>
> When both of them had stepped forward, He said, "Hear now My words: If there is a prophet among you, I, the LORD, will reveal Myself to him in a vision; I will speak to him in a dream. But this is not so with My servant Moses; he is faithful in all My house. I speak with him face to face, clearly and not in riddles; he sees the form of the LORD.
>
> Why then were you unafraid to speak against My servant Moses?" So the anger of the LORD burned against them, and He departed.
>
> ∞ Numbers 12:4-9 BSB ∞

Chapter 29

MEDITATE UPON YOUR DREAMS AND VISIONS

> And while Peter was earnestly revolving the vision in his mind and meditating on it, the [Holy] Spirit said to him, Behold, three men are looking for you!
>
> ∞ Acts 10:19 AMPC ∞

The major reason why most people fail in life is not because they have no dream or a vision. It is simply that they have been disobedient to the dream or vision.

Dreams and visions—whether conscious or unconscious—are common. We constantly visualize and reflect on our experiences, desires, and fears. Unconscious dreams may arise from fear, ambition, spiritual influence, or divine inspiration. While we may not control these moments, they often occur during rest or deep reflection.

What makes a dream or vision transformative is how we respond to it. Do we prioritize it? Do we allow it to shape our choices and focus?

Dreams and visions can be understood across five timeframes:
- *Past* – reflections and lessons
- *Present* – current awareness and action
- *Future* – hope and direction
- *Unrealizable* – distractions or illusions and catalysts for creativity and growth
- *Eternal* – divine purpose and calling

At their core, dreams and visions are forms of meditation—whether conscious or unconscious. Meditation isn't always a complete, structured process; it's a continual posture of openness and alignment, angling towards a free-flow access to the divine and the sublime. Even Joshua was instructed to meditate "day and night" on God's law (Joshua 1:8), showing that spiritual alignment is always ongoing.

We are all at different stages of conception, development, and actualization. To live purposefully, we must align ourselves with our God-given vision. The best way to do this is through intentional, conscious meditation—reflecting deeply, listening intently, and obeying faithfully.

A Great Example of Meditating on Dreams/Visions

The Apostle Peter had a strange encounter. Peter fell into a trance and saw the heavens open. A large sheet descended, filled with all kinds of four-footed animals, reptiles, and birds. A voice told Peter to kill and eat. Shocked, Peter replied that he had never eaten anything unclean or impure. The voice responded, "Do not call anything impure that God has made clean." This exchange happened three times before the sheet was taken back to heaven.

Earlier than Peter's vision, God had spoken to Cornelius, the centurion, to send people to bring Peter to this Gentile centurion's house. However, the Holy Spirit did not reveal or interpret what Peter had seen and for what purpose he showed it three times. Peter knew that this was a confirmed word just by it being repeated thrice.

> As Peter continued to reflect on the vision, the Spirit said to him, "Behold, three men are looking for you.
>
> ∞ Acts 10:19 BSB ∞

MEDITATE UPON YOUR DREAMS AND VISIONS

The importance of this vision was that it symbolized the breaking down of barriers between Jews and Gentiles, urging Peter to embrace all people. He soon learned that God's love and salvation were for everyone, not just a select group.

To begin to initiate this process, God asked Peter to lay aside his Hebrew tradition of separating themselves from the Gentiles and embrace Gentile believers who accepted the Gospel. As happens with traditions, they are difficult to break free from unless one practices conscious checks and balances to unlatch oneself from them.

This is the whole reason why Paul rebuked Peter in Antioch, as recorded in Galatians 2:11-21. This incident occurred when Peter, who had been eating with Gentile believers, withdrew and separated himself from them after some men sent by James arrived. Paul confronted Peter publicly because his actions were inconsistent with the truth of the Gospel when it comes to fellowship and community belonging.

Other great examples of individuals who experienced dreams and visions are Joseph, Daniel, and John, the beloved disciple.

Reflecting on the lives of Joseph, Daniel, Peter, and John reveals profound lessons on meditating on dreams and visions:

Joseph

Faithfulness and Patience: Joseph's dreams showed him a future of greatness, but his journey included betrayal, slavery, and imprisonment. He remained faithful and patient, understanding that his dreams were part of a divine plan. His story teaches us to trust the process and God's timing.

Integrity: Despite his hardships, Joseph maintained his integrity and moral character, knowing that his dreams were worth the wait.

Meditate on Joseph's Example

1. ***Reflect:*** What dreams or visions have stirred in you since youth? Who has believed in them with you?

2. ***Respond with Grace:*** Treat those who betrayed or abandoned you with grace, knowing that only God assigns roles in your journey.

3. ***Realign:*** If you've strayed from your path, find courage to return. Even in the depths of the dungeon, God's calling sees beyond your current place—to the seat beside kings.

Daniel

Dedication to Prayer: Daniel regularly sought understanding and guidance through prayer. When he received visions, he consistently turned to God for interpretation and clarity. This highlights the importance of seeking divine wisdom in our meditations.

Courage and Resolve: Even when facing danger, Daniel stood firm in his faith. His example encourages us to remain steadfast in our beliefs and convictions, even when our visions challenge us.

Carried as a captive to serve in the service of Nebuchadnezzar, Daniel's faith did not also become captive like he was at first.

Meditate on Daniel's Wisdom & Favor

1. ***Resolve*** to keep your faith unshaken, no matter your environment.

2. ***Seek understanding*** from God concerning prophecies and visions that affect your life and your nation.

MEDITATE UPON YOUR DREAMS AND VISIONS

3. ***Serve God*** first, even when others claim authority over your time, gifts, or influence.

4. ***Receive and steward*** divine wisdom, insight, and favor—not for personal gain, but to reveal the greatness of the God you serve.

****Peter****

Peter was a colorful apostle. One moment he and the disciples are afraid of a ghost that was walking on water and the next moment he steps out of the boat to walk on water toward Jesus. In another instance, he wants Jesus to wash all of him and not just his feet.

Getting too warmed by the fire around people who had a hand in crucifying Jesus, he is rebuked by a rooster crowing three times. Feeling dejected, he went back to fish and caught nothing and he came ashore to eat the fish Jesus was roasting on the fire.

Meditate on Peter's Experiences

1. ***God sees the heart:*** Even when emotions run high, it's the posture of your heart that matters most to God.

2. ***The Holy Spirit transforms:*** The indwelling of the Spirit turned Peter's fear into boldness. What once made him deny Christ became the fire that fueled his fearless witness.

3. ***Embrace elevation with humility:*** When God calls and elevates you, serve with humility. The calling is not for status—it's for service.

4. ***Expect divine encounters:*** Peter's walk with God included visions and audible instructions from the Spirit. Stay open to supernatural guidance.

5. ***Practice reflection:*** In moments of uncertainty, Peter learned to pause and meditate, seeking clarity from God before acting.

John

Spiritual Insight: John's visions in Revelation reveal deep spiritual truths. His ability to receive and record these visions shows the importance of being in tune with the Holy Spirit. Meditating on visions requires a receptive heart and mind.

Perseverance in Faith: Despite the challenging nature of his visions, John remained steadfast in his faith, trusting in the ultimate victory of good over evil.

Even with his eyes gouged out, while at the isle of Patmos, this extraordinary apostle saw the future of the world play out as a prophetic revelation.

Meditate on John's Extraordinary Faith

1. ***Revelation through brokenness:*** John, filled with tears wept wondering who could be able to open the seven seals. He was not seeing the Lamb though slain, yet alive in the midst of the throne. Jesus had been broken and qualified to break the seven seals. How is God using your brokenness?

2. ***Compassion in suffering:*** John stood at the foot of the cross, witnessing Jesus' agony. He embraced Mary as his own mother,

MEDITATE UPON YOUR DREAMS AND VISIONS

later caring for her in Ephesus. His love and loyalty endured beyond the pain.

3. ***Guard your worship:*** Overwhelmed by the grandeur of his visions, John knelt before the angel who revealed them—but was rebuked. His experience reminds us to worship God alone, not His messengers.

4. ***Faith through persecution:*** Around 92 AD, per Tertullian's writings, John was thrown into boiling oil—yet miraculously survived. Unable to silence him, Rome exiled him to Patmos, where he received the book of Revelation.

5. ***Spiritual sensitivity:*** In moments of divine silence, John didn't rush. He meditated, waiting for clarity and direction from the Spirit. His example teaches us to listen deeply and respond faithfully.

Chapter 30

THE DUTIES OF YOUR CALLING MEDITATION

> Practice and cultivate and meditate upon these duties; throw yourself wholly into them [as your ministry], so that your progress may be evident to everybody.
>
> ∞ 1 Timothy 4:15 AMPC ∞

There are assignments we can carry out wholesomely.

There are assignments we can continuously learn to do better. There are duties we can excel at by meditating upon them, even as we carry them out.

Remember the parable of the man who built his house on the sand and the one who built it on the rock. The difference between the two is that one considered the strength and longevity needed for the building to endure in all situations, while the other was simply intrigued by the ease of accessibility of the location and the task at hand.

What Paul is advising Timothy is basic and good, in the sense that he is focusing on what Timothy can readily do.

You can have spiritual progress that is visible to those around you. This is revealed by the manifested fruit in your day-to-day life. Can a man harvest grapes or edible fruit from a thorny bush? We know the answer to this. You can only gather rose flowers and rose seeds from a thorny bush—and carefully too, if you are to avoid getting pricked.

> The heart of the discerning acquires knowledge, and the ear of the wise seeks it out.
>
> ∞ Proverbs 18:15 BSB ∞

MEDITATING THROUGH THE BIBLE

Meditating upon your calling is key to your success. This practice allows you to gain deeper insight into yourself, your calling, and how the two relate. It places you in plain view for self-critique and opens your heart to hear from the Holy Spirit dwelling within you. Meditation is not just reflection—it's a spiritual discipline that aligns your inner life with divine purpose.

To meditate successfully on your calling, avoid getting stuck in the rut of repetitive thoughts that merely offer comfort. Be brutally honest with yourself during your self-assessment. Leave nothing unexamined. Teach yourself the art of challenging self-praising evaluations, especially when you know there's room for improvement. This is not a call to negativity. Celebrate the good, acknowledge progress, and confront failure with the mindset: "I can do better than that." Avoid becoming an enabler of your own poor habits.

If we judge ourselves, we will not fall into condemnation—whether by others or in the courts of heaven. After judging ourselves, the next vital step is repentance for our failures or lackluster performance. Repentance, simply put, is the intentional decision to act differently or behave better than we did in similar past circumstances. It must be more than a verbal declaration of intent; it must be a daily demonstration of change that embodies that declaration.

Mature repentance is not accompanied by excuses for failing to be the embodiment of a transformed life. Paul teaches this as the "I die daily" principle. Without daily repentance, we lack the capacity to receive daily resurrection. Even scientifically, the body is worn down during the day, but sleep renews our energy and zest for life.

The rhythm of sunrise and sunset should be reflected in our lives through regular self-assessment. As you go to sleep, reflect on how your day unfolded. As you rise, declare, "The mercies of the Lord are new every morning." With the opening of your eyes, see God's steadfast love that

THE DUTIES OF YOUR CALLING MEDITATION

cannot be quenched. There is strength in the rising sun. There is rest, reflection, and fellowship with God in the sunset. This is how we cool off for the day. We should not miss the opportunity. Take time to reflect. Take time to fellowship with God.

> The LORD by wisdom hath founded the earth; by understanding hath he established the heavens.
>
> ∞ Proverbs 3:19 KJV ∞

If God, in His infinite wisdom and understanding, crafted the heavens and the earth with precision and purpose, then how can we justify serving Him with spiritual ignorance and blabbering careless speech? Shouldn't our devotion reflect the same depth of insight and reverence that He demonstrated in creation?

It is clear here; that the creation and maintenance of the earthly domain requires wisdom for God and for me and you. To establish both natural and spiritual (heavenly) things we must pursue the understanding of God.

Looking at Proverbs 3:19, I bring to your memory the definition of meditation. See what Paul and the full extent of the scriptures point us to. It is meditation, knowledge, wisdom, understanding, prayer, and worship.

Chapter 31

KNOWLEDGE, WISDOM, UNDERSTANDING & MEDITATION IN LIFE

> For as he thinks in his heart, so is he.
>
> As one who reckons, he says to you, eat and drink, yet his heart is not with you [but is grudging the cost].
>
> ∞ Proverbs 23:7 AMPC ∞

As I conclude the writing of this book, I want to guide the reader toward one of the most evident truths found throughout both the Old and New Testament: the power of our thoughts and inner beliefs profoundly shapes our character and actions. A person's true nature is determined not merely by outward behavior or speech, but by what they think and believe in their heart. In essence, our thoughts influence who we are and how we live.

To succeed and prosper in the things we do—for God and for ourselves—we must pay close attention to our thoughts. They shape how we perceive the world, others, God, and life itself. Our thoughts can either nurture our growth in knowledge, wisdom, understanding, meditation, prayer, and worship, or they can undermine these areas to the point where we lose our spiritual footing and sense of identity.

Knowledge, wisdom, understanding, meditation, prayer, and worship are meant to transform us, making us better than we were moments before. These are not tasks we can outsource, postpone, or ignore. They are personal disciplines, essential to our spiritual development. History shows us that civilizations and kingdoms have collapsed when they failed to evolve with the unfolding revelation of these principles and precepts.

As beings created in the image of God, humanity must not regress. The existence of past injustices like slavery should never be a justification for repeating them. No person, institution, government, or group should be above human laws—nor above God's laws. Respect for life, choice, free will, and freedom must not be compromised. If we truly seek and apply God's knowledge, wisdom, and understanding, we will uphold these values.

The challenge we face today is that many have misunderstood God's identity—along with their own and that of others—and as a result, they promote a distorted form of knowledge, wisdom, and understanding that stands in opposition to the Creator's intent. Those privileged to know God and the truth should continue to illuminate and disperse the darkness.

Consider this: the word "knowledge" appears 172 times in the King James Bible—58 times more than "prayer." The word "wisdom" appears 234 times, 120 more times than "prayer." Including their derivatives, knowledge and wisdom are referenced far more frequently than prayer. This is no accident.

It suggests that while prayer is vital, knowledge and wisdom are foundational to our relationship with God. Would God heed a prayer or a meditation that is lacking the wisdom, knowledge, and understanding that are critical to the acceptability of that prayer or meditation. Psalm 19:14 declares, "Let the words of my mouth and the meditation be acceptable in Your sight, O Lord...". This speaks to the foundation of our words and meditation needing to be acceptable.

There are many ways we communication with God - direct conversation of us as spirits to God, prayer, meditation, worship, praise, and face to face for some who are fortunate like Enoch, Moses, and Abraham. Instances of God speaking to humanity are not only prayer and meditatively and neither should our instances be only prayer and meditation.

God brought the animals to Adam and He waited to see what Adam would name them. This act reveals the depth of knowledge and wisdom God had already imparted to Adam. In this light, knowledge and wisdom are not just

KNOWLEDGE, WISDOM, UNDERSTANDING & MEDITATION IN LIFE

tools—they are integral to how we engage with God. Meditation, in turn, creates the environment where knowledge and wisdom can flourish.

Meditation enhances concentration and focus, making it easier to absorb and retain knowledge. It clears mental clutter, allowing for deeper understanding. Mindfulness helps us stay present and fully engaged, enriching the learning process. Through meditation, we cultivate self-awareness—a cornerstone of wisdom. We begin to understand our thoughts, emotions, and behaviors more clearly. This broader perspective enables us to make balanced decisions, guided not by impulse or greed, but by emotional clarity and discernment.

Paul encourages Timothy to carry out his duties with integrity and devotion (1 Timothy 4:15). The calling and the gift to fulfill it come from God, but the responsibility to act lies with the individual. Whether the task is great or small, the choice to fulfill it faithfully is not determined by the magnitude of the gift, but by the intention behind it.

Life is understood not merely through knowledge, but through experience. Many may know about God through reading, yet that knowledge alone does not guarantee a transformative encounter. To truly know God, we must experience Him—His Spirit dwelling and working within us. The written word is vital, but it must be paired with a living relationship. Why seek God only through letters while ignoring His omniscience and omnipresence? As Jesus said, "God is Spirit" (John 4:24), and our understanding of Him is deepened through spiritual experience.

Do not remain suspended between overflowing knowledge and a life lived beneath its potential. It is like being parched beside a rushing stream, unable to drink. Like a drowning swimmer who cannot open his mouth to breathe, we may find ourselves overwhelmed by what we know, yet unable to live it out. Knowledge alone is insufficient unless it is transformed into meaningful, life-giving experience.

So, I ask you: Are you truly living among the living? Why fear the dead lion? Rise to the hope before you. Your challenge is not insurmountable—it is a pet dog that can be tamed. A dead lion cannot chase you anymore. Wake up, embrace the light, and walk boldly into the life God has prepared for you.

> There is hope, however, for anyone who is among the living; for even a live dog is better than a dead lion.
>
> ∞ Ecclesiastes 9:4 BSB ∞

Not all knowledge is life-giving. Some must be weeded out, especially when it becomes a detriment to living well. The partaking of the fruit from the tree of the knowledge of good and evil introduced decay and death into human experience—reminding us that not all knowledge leads to flourishing. Some knowledge exists to highlight the contrast between the good and the bad.

It is far better to live abundantly, guided by relevant and life-enhancing knowledge, than to possess vast but misaligned knowledge while enduring a life that feels like torment—disconnected from the very truths one has acquired.

So how do we find the balance where knowledge and experience complement each other, leading to a life that is both informed and deeply lived?

Wisdom is the key. It is the bridge between knowing and living. Wisdom discerns which knowledge to embrace, how to apply it, and when to let go of what no longer serves the purpose of life and godliness. It transforms information into insight, and insight into action—leading to a fulfilled and meaningful life.

KNOWLEDGE, WISDOM, UNDERSTANDING & MEDITATION IN LIFE

> But where can wisdom be found? Where does understanding dwell?
>
> ∞ Job 28:12 NIV ∞

Job Chapter 28 and Proverbs 8 are some of my favorite scriptures when it comes to meditating on knowledge, wisdom, and life.

I remember being in high school, reading these two chapters together during study. Tears streamed down my cheeks as revelation and understanding engulfed me. It was not a coincidence to turn my Bible pages on the two chapters in the same night. It was only God's guidance and life changing. I urge you to read them in tandem and see for yourself.

Job 28 asks where wisdom can be found. Wisdom and knowledge are not common occurrences; they are rare. Their natural depositories are a mystery. Though related, knowledge and wisdom have significant distinctions between them, spiritually and naturally.

> I, wisdom, dwell together with prudence; I possess knowledge and discretion.
>
> ∞ Proverbs 8:12 NIV ∞

> Counsel and sound judgment are mine; I have insight, I have power.
>
> ∞ Proverbs 8:14 BSB ∞

MEDITATING THROUGH THE BIBLE

Natural knowledge is just the collection of facts, information, and skills acquired through experience or education. It is the theoretical or practical understanding of a subject. Knowledge without understanding remains abstract, intangible, and theoretical serving no impetus or inspiration. Nature and books are full of it, hidden in plain sight. Understanding, the how and why of making it work brings about better planning, harnessing, and application of that knowledge.

A farmer who knows weather patterns prepares better farming practices throughout the year than one who is moved when it rains.

Biblical knowledge is defined as one's capacity to depart from or overcome evil.

Wisdom, on the other hand, involves the ability to make sound judgments and decisions based on knowledge, experience, and insight. It is the application of knowledge in a practical, thoughtful, and often ethical manner. Wisdom includes having perspective and the ability to discern what is true, right, or lasting. Knowledge brings about awareness and knowing things, while wisdom is the actual application, making that knowledge flesh (alive) and beneficial in more ways.

I do not see a one-size-fits-all answer to how we can have both knowledge and the wholesome experience of life. One thing is evident: put your heart and energy into life and learn how to make it better for yourself and others. There are differences between "knowing" and "life" meditation. Paul was writing to Timothy about practicing and cultivating his duties as a minister of God's Word and about godliness. His advice was for Timothy to actively engage in and develop his skills and responsibilities. Consistent effort is not barren of measurable improvement over time.

To develop both his knowledge and experience, Paul encouraged Timothy to "meditate upon these" duties. Deep reflection and thoughtful consideration of one's responsibilities lead to a better understanding of their significance and purpose. Meditation takes you there.

Complete commitment and passion mean dedicating yourself fully to your duties without holding back. The fruit of such dedication not only validates your efforts but also serves as an inspiration and testament to your commitment.

Simply put, Paul urged the youthful Timothy to pursue the acquisition of information, facts, and skills through experience and education. He encouraged Timothy to practice wisdom, not just knowledge.

Timothy would grow in understanding, awareness, and perception of his calling, not only through head knowledge but also through experiences and interactions with both mankind and God. He learned to respond better to human actions, emotions, relationships, and growth.

Timothy had a mentor in Paul, whose experience was broader. Paul not only possessed knowledge but also had experiences, feelings, and interactions with scholars of his day and with Jesus, who spoke to Paul, urging him not to "kick against the pricks."

Experiencing life involves physical, emotional, social, and spiritual dimensions, which can sometimes be complex for certain knowledge bases to encompass. When life and knowledge seem contradictory, remember the "whatsoever things" that are good to unblock the clog. It is far better to experience joy, overcome challenges, build relationships, and find purpose than to be a prisoner of one's limited knowledge.

In essence, knowing is a part of life, but life itself is a much broader and richer experience that goes beyond mere knowledge. It's about how we apply what we know, how we interact with the world, and how we grow and evolve as individuals.

If knowledge is a treasure and practice is the key to this treasure, how good is your practice at unlocking it? Is your knowledge of God taught by your experience of Him? Even Jesus learned obedience to the Father through the experiences He encountered (things He suffered, witnessed, and did).

This reference does not imply that Jesus compromised His knowledge of who God is and His love. He did not stumble in His faith when faced with challenges. The truth is that the evil one gave up trying to tempt Him with position, influence, and riches.

A Meditation Aligning Knowledge to Life

Here is a meditation I pray will help you align your daily knowledge with a godly lifestyle.

The most nagging nuisances in any believer's life often stem from:

- **Human greed** in the forms of lust of the eyes, the flesh, and the pride of life.
- **Falling away**, complacency, and casualness.
- **Denial and incapacity** to change or shift one's vantage point.

Take a stand for yourself in your faith and before God. If you choose not to, who do you expect will take a stand for you?

KNOWLEDGE, WISDOM, UNDERSTANDING & MEDITATION IN LIFE

Closing Words and Meditation

Here are twelve questions for meditation and self-assessment:

1. What is your true motive in desiring material possessions and wealth?
2. Does your pursuit of these things cause you to compromise your faith?
3. Have you engaged in unethical behavior to obtain them?
4. What cravings, habits, and aspirations occupy your thoughts during meditation?
5. Is there evidence that your cravings are driven by envy or comparison?
6. Do you desire to be at the top, even if it means stepping on or putting others down?
7. Do you excuse jealousy and insecurity, even when you know they are wrong?
8. Are you burdened by an excessive craving for physical pleasure or comfort, ignoring natural, moral, and spiritual boundaries? Gluttony, addiction, and immorality often stem from this.
9. Are you driven by a desire for power, status, or recognition? Do you find satisfaction in appearing superior and demanding admiration?
10. Do you engage in disrespectful or harmful behavior toward others as a means of self-elevation?
11. Have you sacrificed ethics and relationships in your pursuit of success and power?
12. Does your appearance or social standing lead you to project a superficial persona, while lacking genuine relationships?

MEDITATING THROUGH THE BIBLE

These questions, when sincerely considered in meditation—not to deceive oneself or others, but to change for the better—can redirect the course of one's life.

The antidote to any harmful trait is not denial or wishful thinking. Covering a problem is not a solution. Healing its root cause is. Reject any identity rooted in lust or pride. You are not your shortcomings. Instead, cultivate a virtuous identity—one that reflects the person you want God to see when He looks at you. This transformation requires both meditation and intentional, selfless action.

Otherwise, inner virtues left unpracticed are like the ghost of a dead man trying to do good works—haunting rather than healing. You will confuse the onlookers if you outwardly display the devil while inwardly aspiring to sainthood.

God already holds what you seek. Seek Him first—and seek His kingdom life. Kingdom life is not self-centered; it nurtures family, friendships, and meaningful connections, creating a life of reciprocal fulfillment.

In closing, let us continue to elevate and ascend—through gratitude, decluttering, mindful acquisition, and intentional kindness.

Thank you for reading this book.

God bless you more than you can ever fathom.

Shalom.

Selah!

Higgaion!

www.ingramcontent.com/pod-product-compliance
Lightning Source LLC
Chambersburg PA
CBHW060117170426
43198CB00010B/921